The Arizona Divo1
Your Step by Step Guide to
Navigate Arizona Divorce

SCOTT DAVID STEWART, ESQ.

www.sdsfamilylaw.com

Published in 2012 by the Law Offices of Scott David Stewart, pllc, USA

• 777 East Thomas Road, Suite 210, Phoenix, AZ 85014 •
• 3115 South Price Road, Suite 107, Chandler, AZ 85286 •
• 17470 North Pacesetter Way, Scottsdale, AZ 85255 •
• 20470 North Lake Pleasant Road, Suite 107, Peoria, AZ 85382 •

www.sdsfamilylaw.com

FIRST EDITION

ISBN 978-0-9886052-0-6

not participate in or encourage electronic piracy of copyrighted materials. Your support of the author's rights is appreciated.

For information please write: Law Offices of Scott David Stewart, pllc, 777 East Thomas Road, Suite 210, Phoenix, AZ 85014.

DISCLAIMER

The general information in this book is not, nor is it intended to be, specific legal advice. You should consult an attorney for specific legal advice regarding your individual situation. Use this book for informational purposes only.

CONTENTS

DEDICATION

Dedicated to those families struggling through transition, looking for help and guidance, while focusing on the needs, hopes, and dreams of their children.

Author's Note

I wrote *The Arizona Divorce Handbook: Your Step by Step Guide to Navigate Arizona Divorce* as a guide for those who are contemplating the possibilities of divorce. I also want the book to be a valuable resource for those who are already engaged in a pending Arizona divorce action.

As I stress throughout the book, getting a divorce education is essential to achieving the best possible outcome in your case – in divorce, knowledge is power. As you read through the book, you will quickly gain insight into the main issues involved in divorce, which will enable you to make truly informed decisions. The choices you make during the divorce process will have long-term consequences for you, for the other party, and for your children. Preparing for your new life after the divorce necessarily requires advance study and planning for each phase of the dissolution process.

There are legal procedures that are beyond the scope of this book, which I wrote as a comprehensive overview of basic Arizona divorce issues. You are sure to have specific questions particular to your family's circumstances, including concerns about what happens after the divorce when child custody issues arise, such as child relocation and modifications to parenting time.

As you read each chapter, freely visit my law firm's website at **www.sdsfamilylaw.com** and utilize it as a supplementary resource to your studies. You will find an extensive library on divorce, property division, child custody and parenting time, visitation, child and spousal support, domestic violence, and alternative dispute resolution.

Sincerely,

Scott David Stewart

Law Offices of Scott David Stewart, pllc

Phone: 602-548-4600

sstewart@sdslawaz.com

www.sdsfamilylaw.com

Introduction:
The Arizona Divorce Handbook:
Your Step by Step Guide to
Navigate Arizona Divorce

Are you contemplating divorce, but have no clue where to begin? Did your spouse already have you served with a summons and court papers? Are you seriously concerned with protecting your rights? Do you know how custody will be decided for your children? If you have questions like these and others, then this book is the ideal place to begin your Arizona divorce education.

To successfully launch your divorce education, the materials in this book have been organized in such a way as to introduce you to each phase of the divorce process. In **Chapter One (*Divorce: Making the Most Difficult Decision and Carrying It Out*)**, you will get sound information on how best to handle the emotional aspects of divorce, so that you are not overwhelmed with the seriousness of the decisions you must make. Decisions that affect your finances, your lifestyle, your happiness, and the future you hope to provide for your children. I talk about *marriage counseling* and *divorce counseling* and provide an essential to-do list to help you plan and prepare for your divorce.

Also in **Chapter One**, you'll read about Arizona's traditional and covenant marriages and the grounds for divorce necessary to dissolve each. From there, in my roadmap to divorce I'll steer you through an overview of the divorce process – giving you a bird's eye view of what to expect. Whether you have children or not, this first chapter will give you much-needed guidance and direction.

Chapter Two (*Child Custody: Who Gets the Kids?*) covers the basic information you need to know regarding custody of a child. I discuss legal custody and physical custody, visitation, parenting time, and parenting plans. The professional facilitators that parents work with to resolve custody conflicts (mediators, parenting coordinators, and child custody evaluators) are also explained. I've included a segment on the Model Parenting Plan, along with some very important custody tips on what *to do* and what *not to do.*

I've devoted **Chapter Three (*All About Finances: Child Support, Spousal Maintenance*)** to the financial aspects of divorce. So you may begin preparing your case before the divorce petition is even filed, to the greatest extent possible, I've included pre-filing instructions to best protect your assets and rights. What follows is a discussion of child support and how to calculate the amount each parent is expected to contribute. Then I talk about spousal support (spousal maintenance) and retirement accounts like pensions, IRAs, and 401(k)s. Regardless of your financial picture, this information will help you prepare your post-divorce financial picture.

Chapter Four (*Property: Who Gets What and Why?*) covers the division of property. To understand how assets and debts are divided in divorce, you need to understand the distinction between separate property and community property. I also talk about what to do if you want to remain in the marital home when it is community property that must be divided between the spouses. The *separation agreement* is also something that you and your spouse will be working through as part of your divorce. An essential component of any fair and reasonable separation agreement is knowing the value of the property to be settled. Therefore, I've included a discussion on the evaluation process of various assets.

With today's technology and the need to preserve privacy and security, I've devoted **Chapter Five (*Privacy and Security: Why Should You Take Action?*)** to keeping your communications via email and the internet private. The risks of social media networking (yes, there really are risks associated with posting information and images on websites), the importance of protecting personally identifiable information (PII), securing personal information during the divorce and child custody proceedings, and the rise of social media evidence in family law court is a very important subject that you need to know about today! When you and your spouse separate, don't assume they won't look and immediately concern yourself with protecting your accounts and passwords.

Because you need to find the right divorce lawyer to represent you, in **Chapter Six (*Choosing an Attorney: What Should You Look For?*)** I explain what characteristics you should look for in an attorney before you make a hiring decision. Your future and the future of your children will depend in great part on the counsel you choose to represent your interests and protect your rights. Of course, cost is always a factor to consider, but if there is one instance in which "penny wise and pound foolish" is an appropriate maxim, this is it. What you save in legal fees at the beginning may cost you in higher legal fees later, not to mention real losses during the divorce that are simply not recoverable.

Moving on with your life after the divorce is final has its own challenges. Being prepared will help you make that transition and that is what **Chapter Seven (*Life After Divorce: Envision What Your New Life Will Be Like)*** is all about setting goals, making a new life for yourself, changing your estate plan, making your new home your children's home, and much more is covered in this chapter.

Chapter 1

DIVORCE:
Making the Most Difficult Decision
And Carrying It Out

The first step you take in this process may be the most difficult – that is, making the decision to end your marriage. You may have reached a level of frustration so intolerable that you find yourself saying with certainty and conviction, "This marriage cannot go on, I am finished with it." Perhaps you have tried – and tried again for the sake of your children – to remain with your spouse, but nothing meaningful ever seems to change for the better.

Maybe your children are grown and on their own. It's just the two of you now with nothing in common, two separate lives simply existing in the same household. Perhaps you have stayed in a loveless relationship for far too long, and now you simply want out. Or maybe you are just plain tired of it all – tired of the arguments, the deceitfulness, the absenteeism, the behavior.

When one spouse files for divorce while the other spouse desires to remain married, the dissolution process still continues. That is not to say that attempts to reconcile are not encouraged, they most certainly are. For example, following service of process on the respondent-party, there is a mandatory 60-day cooling off period before a final decree of dissolution will be issued.[1] So long as one spouse believes the marriage is *irretrievably broken*, though, the divorce will go forward in the family law court.

You have likely been through many struggles in your marriage. Despite the circumstances that brought you to this point, to the brink of divorce, now is *not* the time for impulsiveness. You need to control your emotions. Now *is* the time for calm, thoughtful, rational planning and clear-headedness. Focus your attention on what is necessary to get through the divorce with the best possible outcome. Envision the future you want for yourself and for your children, and keep those long-term goals foremost in mind throughout the entire dissolution process. When you have clearly defined goals, you won't miss opportunities to achieve them.

---

[1] A.R.S. § 25-329. Waiting period.

How Do People Handle the Emotional Aspects of Divorce?

I know from experience that family law cases can be extremely emotional for the parties and for their children. Everyone reacts differently to the pressures of divorce, but most people will experience some feelings of frustration, anxiety, sadness, grief, mild depression, and anger. Unfortunately for some, the circumstances in the home may erode to the point of volatility, which can result in acts of domestic violence. For others, the intense emotions caused by divorce are almost palpable and may even be traumatic.

To get the results you hope for, approach the divorce process with a balanced state of mind. To maintain that balance, take precautions to minimize the impact of any emotional reactions stemming from your divorce. If counseling will help you get through this turbulent period in your life, then find a counselor sooner rather than later.

Have You Tried Marriage Counseling as a Couple?

Someone you know has probably already suggested that you and your spouse attempt to reconcile differences with the help of a professional marriage counselor. Marriage counseling can help spouses explore the possibility of reconciliation, and may guide them through their current domestic impasse. But did you know that the Superior Court Conciliation Services offers free marriage counseling to many Arizona couples? Either spouse may file a "Petition for Conciliation Counseling" to request this family service regardless of whether a divorce, legal separation, or annulment action is already pending with the family law court.

The course of action the parties choose to take after their conciliation counseling sessions are completed is, of course, entirely up to them. If the couple reconciles, then they will probably have their case dismissed immediately. But if they have only solidified their differences, then they will probably continue on with the divorce. If they have made progress toward resolving their differences, then they could ask the court to suspend further action in the divorce while they continue counseling sessions on their own, outside the court's program.

If you and your spouse can agree to try marriage counseling, I urge you to take the recommended sessions and give that process a fair chance. Even if the divorce continues unabated, you may come to understand each other's points of view just a little better. Ideally, that insight could help you resolve custody, property, and support issues with less conflict. You will be able to go forward with the divorce knowing that you did seek professional help and did try to resolve this marital impasse, but could not.

Are You Prepared for the Emotional Challenges of Divorce?

Divorce can be physically and emotionally draining. There will be times when it depletes your finances, seems to squander your time, wears on your emotions, and requires that you pull strength from deep within to do what you must. In many ways, it is like running a marathon. Like any athletic competition, the participants should train mentally and physically because the stakes are very high (your future). When there are minor children, a parent's ability to manage the stress of divorce while maintaining good mental and emotional health could be determinative in whether that parent gets the custody or parenting time desired. As I said, the stakes are very high (your children's future).

Starting with where you are today and how you feel right at this moment, think about what you will do as part of your daily and weekly routine to stabilize your nerves and improve your outlook. Many individuals will meet with professionals for counseling or join discussion groups of similarly situated people. Both of these activities help divorcing parties learn what to expect and how best to manage what can sometimes be an emotional roller coaster ride. There is no quick fix, of course, and what works for one person will not necessarily translate to your circumstances or personality. But understanding how others reacted and responded to situations (and hearing about what worked and what didn't work for them) may be very useful during the more stressful times of your divorce.

Are you wondering just where you should begin? Always start with the fundamentals. *Strive to achieve a healthier lifestyle during your divorce.* Eating healthfully, avoiding drug or excessive alcohol consumption, exercising regularly, getting eight hours of sleep every night, finding spiritual time – all will help markedly in reducing stress to more manageable levels. But sometimes it takes more than a good diet and frequent exercise to get through the intense emotional aspects of divorce, especially when the conflict level between the spouses is high.

You are going through a turbulent period in your life, a period when your ability to make decisions is crucial to a positive outcome in your case. *Consider meeting with a divorce counselor to help you get through this difficult time.* By participating in divorce counseling sessions early on, especially in the high conflict divorce, a party is better able to sustain a calm and clear head when the pressure is really on. Divorce counseling prepares the spouse for the powerful emotions likely to surface as the legal process unfolds.

Divorce counselors discuss specific coping techniques intended to help the party remain focused on each legal issue and a reasonable outcome, without surrendering to anger, depression, or perhaps worse, apathy. With a qualified divorce counselor, the party learns to manage feelings and sensibly address what is happening in the lawsuit which, in turn, often leads to better results, especially for the children of divorce.

When there is any risk of domestic violence, divorce counseling may be essential to avoiding a violent episode. Not all emotional problems stemming from the high conflict divorce will end in acts of domestic violence against a spouse. But all too often that *is* the result, causing severe physical and psychological harm to the victim. Even though they are not the actual target of spousal violence, observing or overhearing the abuse of a parent can emotionally scar a child – and those scars can last a lifetime.

Consider seeking mental health counseling or therapy when emotional matters spiral out-of-control. Your financial resources may dwindle. Your job or school performance may be disrupted. But when your mental health deteriorates under the stress of divorce, you really need to reach out to people for help. You may not even be aware of how your emotions are influencing you, leaving you out-of-sync with the most important people in your life, including your children.

I have seen many times how intensely emotional some family law cases can become, particularly when parents are battling over child custody. When someone who really knows you tries to get your attention by telling you that "you are just not yourself these days" – *Listen!* Take stock of yourself and take action to improve your emotional well-being, whether that entails meeting with a close friend, church leader, family member, or mental health professional. *Reach out for the help you need!*

With your intellectual and emotional focus captivated by the divorce, you may find yourself easily distracted or detached from the world around you. We've all heard horror stories about the parent who left a child in the car "just for a moment" to dash into the store, only to be distracted once inside having momentarily forgotten about the child, the car, and the blazing Arizona sun. Emotional detachment and mental distraction can lead to tragedy. Make sure that you put your safety and the safety of your children first and foremost. In your everyday parenting, accept that you are under extraordinary stress from the divorce – be mindful of where your children are and what they are doing at all times.

Ready to Begin?
Start by Assembling Your Family's Information

Once that decision to end the marriage is firmly made, start planning for the legal aspects of what necessarily follows. As preparation for any divorce, here are seven "to do" steps to get you started on the right track:

1. Prepare your complete financial picture.

2. Set up your own bank account.

3. Take precautions to protect your privacy and security.

4. Prepare for custody of your children.

5. Prepare an inventory of all your personal property.

6. Prepare your contact list of important people.

7. If you really want to keep the house, then don't be the one to leave.

Are you ready to get started preparing for your divorce?

Prepare Your Complete Financial Picture

You will need to provide a complete family financial picture and the more supporting documentation you can gather, the better. Were you planning to move out of the marital home? Then make copies of everything you need for your case before you leave! Once you are gone from the premises, returning to retrieve financial information often leads to complications, delays, and expenses that could have been avoided. If there is any potential for domestic violence, then *do not put yourself at risk of harm* to retrieve records. Instead, discuss the situation with your attorney who will decide how best to proceed.

You will need copies of all your financial information, preferably going back at least 12 months. Here is a checklist of the financial documents you should copy for your case:

- Pay stubs and income verifications
- State and federal tax returns for the prior two reporting years
- Vehicle certificates of title and any loans thereon
- Real property and any mortgages, deeds of trust, or land contracts thereon

- Credit card and charge card accounts
- Insurance policies (note beneficiary designations)
- Investment accounts
- Pension and retirement accounts
- Bank and credit union accounts
- Business operations records

Think of this evidence gathering as taking a "snapshot" of everything financial for your records. If you are unsure whether a certain document is relevant to your case, do not hesitate to copy it anyway. Leave it to your attorney to decide how best to utilize the information, if at all. And if you cannot find specific files, make sure to locate the account numbers (you can order a credit report to fill-in important account details).

You will need to prepare a *budget* that reflects your new living situation. If you are a parent with minor children, then make sure to include all anticipated child-related expenses in that budget as well.

You need to protect this information, so store the copies and any related documents in a secure place that is not accessible by your spouse, such as a safe deposit box that is in your name only.

Set Up Your Own Bank Account

You are beginning a new life, one independent of your spouse. To get started, you need to open a new bank account in your name only – this will be a separate financial account from that of your spouse. Under Arizona's marital property laws, you may take your half of the marital community's cash and direct deposit that amount into your new account.

Take Precautions to Protect Your Privacy and Security

You need to think in terms of protecting your security now, so change the passwords on all of your financial accounts. Change all of your existing email account passwords, too. (But save any emails from your spouse or from others that are relevant to your divorce.) For privileged communications with your attorney, and there will be many, the best course of action is to open a new secure email account in your name only. And if you suspect at any time that the other party has somehow managed to acquire your password, then change it immediately and notify your attorney of the possible privacy breach.

Be very cautious and extremely conservative in your use of social media websites like Facebook and MySpace before, during, and after your divorce. With online social media networking, you need to take extra precautions to protect your privacy and your reputation. Your online social media presence will be highly scrutinized during the divorce. Always be mindful that *what you post may be used against you as evidence in a family law case!* My advice? Think about logging off altogether until after the divorce is final. Even after the divorce is final, however, any online lack of decorum could easily come back to haunt you later in a child custody matter.

To protect your safety, security, and privacy, you should also change the passcode or password on your alarm systems. If you do not have an alarm system in your home and are concerned with safety (even if only because you are unaccustomed to living alone), then consider a professional alarm installation by a security company in your area.

Prepare for Custody of Your Children

Parents who divorce are required to create an in-depth parenting plan for the care of their children. Start keeping a parenting journal to calendar and note what is happening on a daily, weekly, and monthly basis regarding each of your children. It is a lengthy process, but you can begin by thinking through everyone's schedules: school, extra-curricular activities, holidays, doctor visits, your job schedule and the other parent's work hours. Everyone's schedule must be coordinated and charted out for the entire year as part of your proposed parenting plan.

You need to make decisions about who the children will live with. Will there be shared custody? How often will the children be visited by the noncustodial parent? How will the children's expenses be paid? Decisions must also be made over the children's healthcare, education, religion and welfare. If you will not be seeking primary physical custody, then you should concern yourself with maximizing your parenting time and staying involved in your kids' daily lives.

Prepare an Inventory of All Your Personal Property

You must inventory *all* of your personal property. I recommend that you take photographs or video record the community property, as well as the overall condition of your marital home. To prepare an accurate inventory, it may be helpful to list the personal property in each room: kitchen, bedrooms, family room, bathrooms, laundry room, exercise room, media room, garage, and so on.

In Arizona, community property includes all assets that you and your spouse accumulated during the marriage. Separate property, by contrast, includes any property owned by either of you before the marriage, or that either of you acquired by gift or inheritance during the marriage. As you compile your inventory of personal property, list the item description and jot down a "C" (for community) or "S" (for separate) next to each entry for later reference.

If you plan to leave the marital home, then take the things that are irreplaceable to you, such as photographs of your children and family keepsakes. Don't leave these items in trust with your spouse, you may never get them back. Instead, make copies and take photograph of the items, then place them in your personal safe deposit box (or store them appropriately at some other secure location).

Prepare Your Contact List of Important People

With your life about to undergo a major change, this is not the time to lose contact with those who are involved with your family's life. These are important people with whom you need to stay connected during and after the divorce. Prepare a complete list of telephone, address, and email information for your family's doctors, teachers, accountants, financial planners, insurance agents, counselors, professional advisors, day care centers, employers, pastors, family members, neighbors, and so on.

If You Really Want to Keep the House, Then Don't Be the One to Leave.

Whether or not to stay in the home is a very important decision requiring careful consideration, even more so when you have minor children. If you really want to remain in the marital home during and after the divorce, then don't move out.

Before you commit to staying or leaving, though, take a few moments to reflect. What is the condition of the residence? Does it need major repairs? Are you able to devote the time and money necessary to maintain the house on your own? How closely tied are you and your children to the community? Is the home in a safe neighborhood? Are the schools good? Will your children be bussed long distances? What are the employment opportunities for you? What is the possibility of selling the home? Are you likely to make money, lose money, or break even if the house is sold? Is there more desirable housing available elsewhere?

A word on domestic violence. There is one very important exception to staying in the home during and after the divorce. Whenever there is potential for domestic violence, *put your safety and the safety of your children first and leave the marital home* for a safer environment or safe house. If you or your children are threatened with domestic violence or abuse, immediately contact your local police or county sheriff.

Getting Your Divorce Education

No matter which spouse files the petition for dissolution, the divorce process can be a challenging experience. Whether you were surprised by the divorce or saw it coming long ago, the emotional, financial, and children's issues will impact you significantly. Just about every aspect of your personal life will be discussed during the divorce. Getting a basic divorce education will make handling your own considerably easier. Not easy, but certainly easier. Once again, we start with the fundamentals.

In the legal sense, divorce terminates the marriage contract between husband and wife, giving each the right to marry some other person after the divorce is final. Our Arizona Superior Courts have subject matter jurisdiction over family law matters, including annulment, legal separation, divorce, child custody, child support, property division, and spousal maintenance.[2] The divorce will divide the couple's marital assets and debts, will determine child custody and parenting time, and will establish child support and spousal support.

What Are Legal Grounds for an Arizona Divorce?

Arizona's no fault divorce laws allow the courts to legally dissolve a marriage without allegations of fault or marital misconduct – this takes the blame out of divorce. Unlike some states, there is no requirement in Arizona that the spouses be separated for a specified period of time before the divorce can be finalized. Either party may obtain a divorce without the consent of the other spouse. The no fault ground for divorce is that the marriage is "irretrievably broken" with no reasonable expectation of reconciliation.[3] Once that is established, the court can dissolve the civil marriage contract between a man and a woman. However, there is another Arizona marriage that does require certain

---

[2] Arizona Constitution, Article VI § 14.

[3] A.R.S. § 25-316. Irretrievable breakdown; finding.

allegations and proofs before the marriage may be dissolved by the court – the covenant marriage.

What Is Arizona's Covenant Marriage?

The covenant marriage made its way into Arizona law in 1998. Additional requirements and formalities are involved when a couple enters into (or exits out of) a covenant marriage. Premarital counseling, for example, is a marriage prerequisite and the couple's marriage license reflects their covenant election. The court can only dissolve a covenant marriage[4] when the party seeking a divorce alleges and proves that at least one of the following is true:

- *The other spouse committed adultery.*
- *The other spouse was convicted of a felony and sentenced to imprisonment or death.*
- *The other spouse abandoned the marital home for at least a year.*
- *The other spouse committed domestic violence or emotional abuse.*
- *For at least two years, the spouses were separated continuously without reconciliation.*

---

[4] A.R.S. § 25-903. Dissolution of a covenant marriage; grounds.

- *For at least one year, the spouses were separated continuously without reconciliation after a decree of legal separation was obtained.*
- *The other spouse habitually abused drugs or alcohol.*
- *Both spouses agree to dissolve their covenant marriage.*

The sixth ground for divorce of a covenant marriage referred to a *decree of legal separation*. Legal separation does everything but terminate the civil marriage contract between the husband and wife. The marriage is still determined to be irretrievably broken and the parties still address issues of child custody, support, and property division. If one party objects to the legal separation, then the court cannot proceed further – the spouses either get divorced or stay married. Unlike divorce, the spouses who are legally separated by judicial decree cannot marry other people because they remain legally married to each other.

Drive-By View of Arizona's Divorce Procedure

The divorce process can seem rather daunting at first, but as you read through each chapter in the Divorce Handbook it will become less and less of a mystery. Here is a drive-by view of the main steps you will encounter in your Arizona divorce:

Step 1: *Petition for Dissolution of Marriage*. Filing this petition asks the court to dissolve the marriage and is the document initiating the divorce proceedings.

Step 2: *Summons and Response*. This is formal notice to your spouse (the other party) of your intention to pursue court action to obtain a legal divorce. The other party's response is his or her acknowledgement that the divorce procedure has begun.

Step 3: *Motions*. These are formal requests for the court to order some type of action before the trial. In situations involving domestic abuse, for example, it is not uncommon for a motion for a protective order, or restraining order, to be filed.

Step 4: *Discovery.* This phase of the divorce allows each side to gather information and evidence in support of their legal arguments. The tools of discovery include interrogatories, depositions, requests for production, requests for admission, and so on.

Step 5: *Hearings and Temporary Orders.* Sometimes there are questions or situations that need to be temporarily resolved before the final divorce agreement is reached or ordered by the court. If the parties cannot agree on where their children should live during the divorce process, for example, then they may ask the judge during the hearing to decide for them. Generally, the court's temporary orders will remain in effect until the final decision is made at the end of the divorce.

Step 6: *Trial.* This is a critical court appearance before the judge where the case will be decided. The trial may include witnesses, friends, financial experts, psychologists, as well as the submission of other types of evidence including financial records. When parties reach agreement on all issues in their divorce, the necessity of a trial may be avoided.

Step 7: *Final Decree of Divorce.* The final decree of dissolution is a judgment, a legal statement of the judge's rulings on all the issues in question during the trial including child custody and visitation, child support, spousal maintenance, and property division.

As you read through the following chapters, it is only natural that you should start developing questions pertinent to your family's unique circumstances. To continue your divorce education beyond the pages of this book, I encourage you to visit my law firm's website at www.sdsfamilylaw.com for additional family law information. With free videos, divorce webinars, downloadable apps, and *Divorce Talk Radio*, the Law Offices of Scott David Stewart's website covers all aspects of Arizona divorce, child custody and child support, property division, spousal maintenance, domestic violence, and mediation in divorce. You can also sign up for our free monthly *Arizona Divorce Newsletter* with its current events and helpful advice on family law.

Chapter 2

CHILD CUSTODY:
Who Gets the Kids?

If you and your spouse have children, then child custody and parenting time are the most important family decisions you will be making in your divorce. Take a moment now to visualize yourself raising the children after the divorce is final.

Have you thought about what your kid's lives will be like? What kind of relationship do you hope to have with your children? What kind of relationship will your children have with the other parent? If your child is disabled, how will you ensure that his or her special needs are met? In the event of remarriage, how do you believe your children should be treated by a step-parent? When your child graduates from high school, will both parents assist with the cost of vocational training or college tuition?

The answers to these and related custody questions are often emotionally charged, and that is to be expected. We are talking about your kids' futures, after all.

Staying on top of the child custody issues in your divorce will require considerable effort on your part, so start preparing yourself immediately. You need to learn about Arizona's custody laws; what the court will require from you and the other parent; what your respective parental rights are; and what your legal options may be. In this chapter, I will start you off with a short introduction followed by a discussion of legal custody, physical custody, and parenting plans.

Introducing Child Custody

Many parents arrive at my law office with only a vague idea of what child custody is all about. Unless they have dealt with these issues in a previous family law case, parents are often in the dark over how Arizona's courts handle custody matters. Not only do people struggle with the legal terminology, they are commonly under the misguided impression that child custody laws are uniform from state to state, which is not so.

In some states, for example, a child may choose the parent he or she wants to reside with. In Arizona, the court is required to "consider... [t]he wishes of the child as to the custodian" in determining what is in the best interests of that child. But the child has *no right to decide* which of his parents will be the custodian.

Although not a common practice in Arizona, the family law judge does have discretion to interview the child *in camera* to hear the child's position on custody. Typically, the court will refer the child interview to *conciliation services* and have them submit a report to the court regarding the child's wishes. The judge may also consider the parents' testimony on *what they believe* their child's wishes for custody are. More commonly, though, the court will be guided by the professional opinions of mental health experts in deciding what is in the child's best interests.

This may also surprise you, but there is no presumption in the law that a child's mother will get custody. Instead, it is the parent who is the child's day-to-day caregiver (mother or father) that carries great weight with the court in deciding custody matters.

What Every Parent Should Know About Legal Custody

Whenever I begin discussing "who gets custody" with a parent, I start the conversation with a clear description of the two basic divisions – that is, the difference between *legal custody* and *physical custody.*

Think of *legal custody* as the cornerstone of parental decision-making over the child. The parent with legal custody has authority to determine how important decisions over the child will be made. These are decisions over many essential matters, such as the child's healthcare, education, and the faith the child is brought up in. If one party is granted *sole legal custody*, then only that parent has authority to determine how those important decisions will be made. Under *joint legal custody*, which is the most common arrangement in Arizona, both parents retain equal decision-making authority over these important child-rearing matters.

What Does it Mean to Have Physical Custody?

Many parents are confused by the term *physical custody* which refers to the amount of time the child will spend with each parent. With joint physical custody, neither parent is designated the *primary residential parent*. However, in those circumstances where one parent has significantly more parenting time than the other, then a *primary residential parent* may be designated, allowing that parent to make day-to-day decisions concerning the child. Designation as the primary residential parent may affect legal decisions, too, such as the child's school.

What Does it Mean to Have Parenting Time?

What parenting time encompasses is the regular parenting/visitation schedule for the child, as well as holiday parenting time, summer parenting time, and any other special parenting time, including vacation and special occasions. Parents are encouraged to work together and create their own parenting schedule so they can avoid the expense and uncertainty of contested custody litigation.

Learning the Essentials of Legal Custody

The place to begin with Arizona's legal custody framework is A.R.S. § 25-403 which gives the court discretion to order *sole* or *joint custody* (neither of which is favored by presumption at law, by the way). And although many parents believe the mother has the custodial advantage, the court cannot prefer one parent over the other based on the party's sex.

Whenever custody is contested, the court must "make specific findings on the record about all relevant factors and the reasons for which the decision is in the best interests of the child." Again we look to A.R.S. § 25-403 and its laundry list of relevant factors to consider when determining whether joint custody is in a child's best interests. Some of the factors considered in every custody matter include:

- *The parents' and child's wishes;*
- *The child's interrelationships with family members and others;*
- *The mental and physical condition of everyone involved;*
- *The parent likely to facilitate a meaningful relationship between the child and the other parent;*
- *The acting primary caregiver;*
- *The occurrence of any coercion, duress, domestic violence, or false reporting of abuse in the custody case.*

Be mindful that not every parent will get custody, legal or physical. It probably will not surprise you to learn that a parent's domestic violence or child abuse is considered to be contrary to the child's best interests. The court will not award joint custody when a preponderance of the evidence supports a finding that a party has a significant history of domestic violence.

Similarly, a parent's conviction history of drug offenses in the prior year creates a rebuttable presumption that sole or joint custody with that offending parent is also contrary to the child's best interests. And a party who is a registered sex offender or who was convicted of murdering the other parent will not be granted sole or joint custody (legal or physical) or unsupervised parenting time. The exception being if the court, after considering credible evidence, makes specific findings that the parent in question poses "no significant risk to the child."

What Every Parent Should Know About Physical Custody

Whenever there is a minor child involved in a couple's break-up, major decisions over physical custody must be made in the child's best interests. In Arizona, if parents seek *joint legal custody*, then they are expected to cooperate in creating a written *parenting plan* for their child. Should you share joint custody with your spouse, your parenting plan will provide a defined, predictable custody arrangement that delineates the terms of access that both of you must abide by and upon which your child depends.

The parenting plan is integrated into the court's child custody orders, which renders it fully enforceable against both parents. With custody orders in place, the parties are not reliant upon each other's goodwill to maintain and build healthy relationships with their child.

As you may have surmised already, a cooperative spirit is not always forthcoming in a divorce or legal separation, not even when a child's future hangs in the balance. Should any element of the plan be disputed or the parties remain intransigent, the family law judge will resolve any stubborn, outstanding issues and decide how the parties will go about parenting their child. Just knowing that an outsider, the judge, could control the family's parenting decisions is often sufficient incentive for people to work through their differences of opinion and concentrate on the needs of their child.

Custody orders are not something judges are eager to change without a show of good cause. As it is, the custody decree cannot be modified for a full year following its entry, which is yet another reason why the parenting plan must be thorough. Only with a motion alleging a dangerous environment will the court consider modifying child custody sooner. Such a request must include affidavits, or sworn statements, sufficient to persuade the judge that the child may be in a dangerous environment that could have serious physical, mental, emotional, or moral consequences.

Are You Prepared for Parenting Time?

As previously discussed, physical custody is the amount of time that a child spends with each parent. But there is a lot more to a parenting plan than scheduling what time one parent picks the kids up or what day the other drops them off.

Parenting time is the parent's right to have the child physically with him or her. During parenting time, the mother or father has the right and responsibility to make routine day-to-day child care decisions. (Decisions consistent with the important determinations made by the parent with sole legal custody.) A parent who has not been granted custody is still entitled to frequent, continuing contact with his or her child and reasonable parenting time.

To stay on the right track in the best interests of your child, make sure to use this checklist of parenting time do's and don'ts:

DO be prompt, yet flexible, with parenting time exchanges.

No parent should be habitually late for parenting time exchanges, but sometimes delays are unavoidable. When you cannot pick-up or drop-off the child as scheduled, communicate that to the other parent.

DO maximize your parenting time.

When spending time with your child, make sure you engage in meaningful activities. Be intentional with the time you spend together by planning ahead. Arrange for both structured and unstructured age-appropriate activities.

DO make your home your child's home.

Children need a place of their own to feel secure and in control. If possible, provide the child with a separate bedroom or a special personal space somewhere in the home, perhaps a corner desk in a shared bedroom or an area in the living room just for the child's toys, books, and furniture.

DO help your child establish friends in the neighborhood.

Encourage your child's involvement in the community and in school. Establish normal daily, weekly, and monthly routines; children feel more in control when they know what is expected of them and what to expect from others.

DO keep a parenting journal.

Keep accurate, detailed records of your parenting time (dates, times, activities, events, etc.). Record information about your interactions with the other parent. A parenting journal will be very useful in refreshing your memory should a custody problem or dispute arise.

DO share information with the other parent.

Parents must share critical information, such as telephone numbers and addresses. Volunteer information regarding your child's educational, medical, religious, and extracurricular activities. Always document these events and activities in your parenting journal.

DO maintain telephone access with your child.

Maintain daily telephone communication with your child. Establish a set time to call your child and consistently call everyday at that agreed upon time. If you have physical custody, allow the child to have frequent, private, meaningful telephone conversations with the other parent.

DON'T be carefree about significant others.

Use considerable discretion in introducing any significant other to your child. Most child custody evaluators caution against introducing new parental figures into a child's life prematurely.

DON'T engage in parental alienation.

Parental alienation occurs when a parent engages in conduct that attempts to negatively influence the child toward the other parent. In child custody litigation, there is no bigger mistake than to engage in this conduct.

DON'T use your child as a messenger or case manager.

A child should never be told to deliver messages to the other parent or to spy on the other parent. Don't interrogate your child over the other parent's activities, either. Don't allow the child to arrange visitation, change visitation, or cancel visitation – the child is not the case manager.

DON'T confuse parenting time with child support.

Parenting time is not contingent upon the payment of child support. You'll read more about this in Chapter 3's discussion on child support.

Can Either Parent Seek Custody?

Either parent may seek to gain primary physical custody of the child. Once a custody action is initiated, the court begins assessing what is in the best interests of the child and may award joint custody over either parent's objections. The mother or father may request temporary custody orders to address parenting time during pendency of the action, before a trial and permanent orders are forthcoming.

When the court is asked to order joint custody, which is shared parenting, both parents must agree to such joint custody; joint custody must be in the best interests of the child; and the parents must agree to submit a written parenting plan to the court.

If you do not seek primary physical custody of your child, do make sure to maximize your parenting time.

What Goes into a Proposed Parenting Plan?

Given how emotionally invested parents are in their children, child custody disputes can be intense. Negotiating a reasonable parenting plan may be more difficult than with other divorce issues. But this is not a competition over who wins the "grand prize." No matter how challenging this process is, the focus of these discussions must always be on what is best for the child.

Think of the parenting plan as a guidebook or blueprint delineating how the child will be parented after the divorce. Once completed, the plan will help both parents and child adjust to life after the divorce in positive ways.

The proposed plan is filed with the court and must be approved by the judge. When you begin working on your parenting plan, look at A.R.S. § 25-403.02(A) which requires that you include the following six provisions at a minimum:

1. *Each parent's rights and responsibilities for the personal care of the child and for decisions in areas such as education, health care, and religious training.*
2. *A schedule of the physical residence of the child, including holidays and school vacations.*
3. *A procedure by which proposed changes, disputes, and alleged breaches may be mediated or resolved, which*

may include the use of conciliation services or private counseling.

4. *A procedure for periodic review of the plan's terms by the parents.*

5. *A statement that the parties understand that joint custody does not necessarily mean equal parenting time.*

6. *A statement that each party has read, understands, and will abide by the notification requirements of § 25-403.05(B)[regarding convicted or registered sex offenders or dangerous crimes against children]...*

Arriving at an effective parenting plan takes careful thought, negotiation, and a genuine desire to set aside differences for the child's benefit. When you begin working on your parenting plan, consider downloading a copy of *Arizona's Guide for Parents Living Apart* from the Arizona Supreme Court's website at www.azcourts.gov. The guide is free and includes model parenting time plans to help you schedule parenting time for a child of any age, from infant to teenager.

It's All in the Plan: Details, Details, Details

All of the situations that parents deal with every day regarding their child should be addressed in the parenting plan. Details on how the parties will share holiday and vacation time. Details on which parent will have what child-rearing responsibilities. When you are ready to get started, here is a checklist of parenting decisions that need to be made and included in your proposed plan:

- Which parent will be designated as having legal custody?
- Which parent will be designated as having physical custody?
- Who will be responsible for the child's medical, dental, and optical care?
- What will be the parenting time schedule for weekdays, holidays, and vacations?
- How will future problems or conflicts relating to the parenting plan be resolved?
- How will the parents decide where the child will attend school?
- What will be the day care arrangements?

- Which parent will take the child to school and pick up the child from school?
- Where and when will parenting time exchanges take place?
- How will the parents ensure the child's safety?
- How will the parents prevent their conflict from harming the child?
- How will each parent maintain a nurturing environment for the child that is safe and stable?
- How will the child's basic needs (food and clothing), supervision, and emotional well-being be provided for?
- How will each parent help the child maintain a positive, healthy relationship with the other parent, and with others in the family and community?
- How will the child's social, academic, athletic, or other activities be supported (within the parent's financial means)?
- How will extraordinary expenses be handled?
- What will be the notification requirements of any anticipated change to the child's residence?

As you can see, parenting plans are meant to cover every aspect of child-rearing. Although modifications are sometimes needed as circumstances change, a comprehensive parenting plan – with all the details and contingencies worked out in advance – diminishes the need for court intervention later on, when the inevitable bumps in life's road happen.

What Happens When Custody Orders Are Violated?

Once custody orders are in place, what happens when a parent deviates significantly from the parenting plan?

There are many ways one parent or both parents can violate child custody orders. Maybe one parent refuses to drive the child to the other parent's home on Sunday evenings, as required by the plan exchange rules. Perhaps the party takes the child on Thanksgiving when it is the other parent's turn under the plan.

Always bear in mind that deviating from the parenting plan is a deviation from the court's child custody and parenting time orders and the decision to do so can be a costly one. When custody orders are violated, the court may find a parent in contempt, may order that missed parenting time be recovered, and may assess court costs, civil penalties, and attorney fees against the violator. Family law judges frequently order parties back into mediation to resolve their conflicts, too, and they can assess cost at the violating parent's expense.

Mediators, Parenting Coordinators, and Child Custody Evaluators

Child custody is among the most contentious areas of family law, so there is a distinct possibility that your divorce could involve disputed custody or parenting time issues. (Even if you and your spouse seem to be in agreement now, there is always the potential for disagreement later on.) When the level of conflict between parents is so intense and persistent that they are unable to cooperate and make decisions about their child's future, then it is time to bring in a dispute resolution facilitator to help break through the impasse.

Ordinarily, we rely on three different child custody professionals to help the parties arrive at a custody arrangement that, first, is best for the child and, second, serves each parent's independent interests. Any one of the following dispute resolution facilitators, or all of them, may be utilized in your custody matter: the *mediator*, the *parenting coordinator*, and the *child custody evaluator*.

Why Mediation?

Through mediation, parents work toward agreement on the disputed child custody issues presented to the mediator. If the parties reach agreement through mediation, it is very possible that a custody trial will be unnecessary. The mediated agreement is signed by both parents and submitted to the judge who, assuming there is no objection, will sign the order. By reaching a mediated agreement, the parties maintain control of their child custody arrangement. And if the parties do not reach agreement, the court will decide what is in the best interests of the child and dictate the custody terms to the parents.

How Can a Parenting Coordinator Help?

When conflict persists between parents and interferes with their custody decision-making, involving a parenting coordinator may be the best course of action. Without advocating for either parent, the coordinator meets with both to discuss their concerns about the parenting plan. An experienced coordinator will skillfully and tactfully weave counseling, parent-education, and alternative dispute resolution (ADR) techniques into these sessions. While facilitating negotiations, the coordinator assists the parents in reaching a fair settlement – one that is in their child's best interests and still satisfies as many of their individual needs as is practical. The parenting coordinator reports back to the court with recommendations. Either party may object to the coordinators recommendations. The court will approve, modify, or reject those recommendations or may set the matter for hearing.

Why Involve a Child Custody Evaluator?

The child custody evaluator will, after thorough investigation and inquiry, make custody and parenting time recommendations to the court. For the purpose of making a recommendation in the child's best interests, the evaluator interviews the parents, the child, and other family members, and reviews documents and records regarding the child. The evaluator then submits a detailed report to the court with recommendations for legal custody, physical custody and parenting time. Should a custody trial become necessary, be aware that the custody evaluator's report will be very influential with the court.

Have You Attended the Parent Information Class?

In every Arizona case involving child custody, specific parenting time, or child support, both parties must complete a parent information course within 45 days of the initial court filing. This class educates parents on the impact their separation and divorce may have on the emotional well-being of their child.

Statistics bear out that parents are more capable of cooperating with each other for their child's benefit after they have taken this parent education class. The program also minimizes return visits to the courthouse to resolve future parenting disputes. Check with the Clerk of the Superior Court where your case is filed to get the details of where and when the course is offered. After you finish the parenting class, you will need to file your certificate of completion with the court.

Ensuring that you understand all of the responsibilities associated with child custody is essential to resolving disputes, to avoiding protracted ligation, and to reducing the likelihood of a petition to modify child custody later on.

Chapter 3

ALL ABOUT FINANCES: Child Support and Spousal Maintenance

In this chapter, I introduce two very important financial issues in divorce, namely child support and spousal maintenance (spousal support). In the next chapter, I discuss those financial issues relating to the division of property, including retirement accounts, IRAs, 401(k)s, and other valuable assets. For now, though, let's get started with the two basic support issues in divorce.

What Every Parent Should Know About Child Support

In the previous chapter, I discussed many core concepts relating to child custody in Arizona, including legal and physical custody and parenting plans. *In every child custody case there will be a determination of child support.*

Before I get into the nuts and bolts of child support, however, there is one common misconception to dispel – the connection between parenting time and child support.

Access to Your Child Is Not Dependent Upon Timely Payment of Child Support

A parent's access to his or her child is not contingent upon the timely payment of child support. Consequently, the custodial parent cannot lawfully interfere with the other party's visitation or parenting time, even when child support arrearages are mounting.

On its face this may seem unfair, especially to the frustrated parent who religiously follows the parenting plan while the other falls even further behind on child support. But parenting plans and parenting time relate to custody, and child custody and child support are two distinct legal matters. It would violate the terms of the parenting plan for the custodial parent to refuse access and parenting time because the other parent is delinquent in the payment of child support.

As you learned in Chapter 1, the court-approved parenting plan includes the terms and conditions that govern the parties' conduct regarding their children's custody. If one party violates the terms of the parenting plan, the other party (yes, that would be the one behind in child support) may *protect the child* by petitioning the court. Interfering with parenting time harms the child by hindering his or her relationship with a parent. Obstructing parenting time also interferes with the non-custodial parent's right of access to the child. Consequently, attempts to enforce the other parent's support obligation by withholding parenting time will, in all likelihood, result in a contempt action against the party who prevented access. The judge in the family law case will not condone any obstructive actions taken by a parent in retaliation for the other's nonpayment of child support.

One last thought. Please refrain from talking about child support issues in the presence of your son or daughter. Placing a price on children risks making them feel their only value is in the collection of support money. Problems and discussions involving child support are for adults only – that is, for the Court, the parties, and their attorneys.

How Is Child Support Calculated?

As with all other states, Arizona's child support guidelines are used to determine how much child support each parent will contribute. Support is based on specific criteria relating to the parents' income and the number of children residing in the home. *The court will not take into account the parents' living expenses in setting child support!* Only the parents' income, the parenting time exercised by the non-custodial parent, and the expenses for the child's daycare, health insurance, and special needs are considered. Unless there are exceptional circumstances (such as an autistic child's educational needs), the court will follow the amount suggested by the guidelines.

As a parent, you need to know how support will be ordered for your child or children. Because application of the *Arizona Child Support Guidelines* is mandatory in every family law case with minor children, this is one reasonably predictable area of divorce. To get an idea of the support obligation in your case and to begin budgeting, use the free child support calculator on my law firm's website (www.sdsfamilylaw.com). You can also download our free Arizona child support calculator apps for your iPhone (shop iTunes) and Android (shop Google play) mobile devices.

For the most part, the child support guidelines work well for families. The more common difficulties occur when a parent has self-employment income or cash-based income. In those circumstances, income may fluctuate significantly from month-to-month or even from week-to-week. Otherwise, calculating support is simply a matter of plugging in the parties' income, answering a few questions about the children and child-related expenses, indicating how many other children are in the household, and getting an estimated monthly child support obligation for each parent.

Go ahead and run the numbers through the child support calculator to see what your figures turn out to be. Just make sure before you start that your numbers are accurate and not just estimates. Best to first list expenses like children's health insurance premiums, daycare, and extraordinary expenses for any particular child. If you enter grossly inaccurate data, you will get incorrect and fairly useless results. So enter realistic figures when you are working with any support calculator.

Here is a checklist of the information you should have at your fingertips when you are ready to work through the child support calculator:

- Both parents' gross income
- Spousal maintenance paid or received
- Child's medical, dental, and vision insurance premiums
- Court-ordered child support for children from other relationships
- Expenses for child care and daycare
- Extraordinary expenses for a child
- Additional education expenses for a child
- Number of your children who are age 12 or older
- Month and year of your youngest child's birthday
- Number of parenting time days per year
- Court-ordered arrears paid by the non-custodial parent

In any action involving child support, the amount calculated under the guidelines is presumed to be the amount the court shall order. However, the judge does have discretion to make exceptions when results under the guidelines would be unjust or inappropriate in the circumstances. When exception is taken, the court may deviate from the guidelines by increasing or decreasing the amount of child support.

In Arizona, the court's order must include the exact amount of child support and the date that payments are to begin. The judge will make specific findings for the official record, including each parent's gross and adjusted gross income, the basic and the total child support obligation, the non-custodial parent's proportional share, and any attributed income in excess of the minimum wage. Be mindful that when a child under the support order emancipates, the support does not automatically reduce. To avoid an unintentional overpayment, the non-custodial parent needs to return to court and seek an order modifying child support.

What You Should Know About Child Support Guidelines

The Arizona Child Support Guidelines provide necessary structure and consistency to child support orders.

Taking a look at the guidelines may be helpful in determining each parent's child support obligation, but there is no need to commit the guidelines to memory word-for-word. However, every parent should understand the guideline's seven essential premises:

1. ***The guidelines apply to all children.*** It makes no difference to the calculations whether the parents were married or unmarried when the child was conceived or born; or whether the child is the natural offspring of the parents or was legally adopted.

2. ***Paying child support is a priority financial obligation.*** Financial responsibility for a child trumps the parents' other debts, which are not considered in determining either party's share of child support. (Child support is not a dischargeable debt in bankruptcy, either!)

3. ***Spousal maintenance is determined before child support obligations are established.*** This is because spousal support (alimony) is income to the recipient and must be included in that parent's gross income for child support purposes.

4. ***Every parent has a legal duty to support his or her natural or adopted child.*** The financial support of a step-child is voluntary, however.

5. ***Under some circumstances, the custodial parent may be required to pay child support.*** There is no absolute rule that the non-custodial parent must pay support to the custodial parent. (But more often than not, it works out that way.)

6. ***Child support is calculated on a monthly income basis.*** Adjustments to support are annualized to achieve a monthly figure. This allows for an equal monthly distribution of the cost item over the course of a year.

7. ***Basic child support is capped when the parents' combined adjusted gross income reaches $20,000 per month; and is also capped with the sixth child.*** When there are more than six children, basic support is capped with the sixth child.

The duration of child support is determined by the judge, who will set a termination date in the child support order. Child support is paid until the child reaches age 18, completes high school, becomes self-sufficient, or emancipates. There is one important circumstance, though, when the court may order child support to continue into the child's adulthood.

For the court to order such support, the adult-child must be "severely mentally or physically disabled as demonstrated by the fact that the child is unable to live independently and be self-supporting"; said disability must have manifested during the child's minority.[5]

If your disabled child was already an adult when the divorce was filed or will be an adult by the time your final decree is issued, then you may still seek the child support order. You do not need to obtain a custody or guardianship order before the court can order support for your disabled adult-child.[6] Also, in these special circumstances the court may order support paid to the adult-child directly or to the parent providing for the care.

Parents may agree to additional support payments in excess of the guidelines as well, for example to pay for private school tuition, travel, or summer camp. To be enforceable, the agreement to provide additional support dollars must be written into the parties' separation agreement and included in the court's support order.

---

[5] A.R.S. § 25-320. Child support; factors; methods of payment; additional enforcement provisions; definitions.
[6] *Gersten v. Gersten*, 219 P3d 309 (Ariz.App. 2009).

What About Child Support Enforcement?

When child support payments fall behind, the appropriate course of action for the custodial parent is to seek lawful enforcement of the support order in court. In Arizona, a parent who fails to financially support his or her minor child will be penalized. When the court's support order is violated, the Arizona Department of Economic Security's Child Support Enforcement office will pursue most claims.

For violating a child support order, the court in contempt proceedings may order the non-custodial parent jailed and fined; may suspend a driver's license, professional or occupational license, and recreational license; may seize the parent's assets and intercept state tax refunds. And when the non-payment is deliberate, the non-custodial parent who "knowingly fails to furnish reasonable support" may be prosecuted for a class 6 felony under Arizona law.[7] Federal prosecution for willful non-payment of child support is also possible when a non-custodial parent and his or her child reside in different states.[8]

---

[7] A.R.S. § 25-511. Failure of parent to provide for child; classification.
[8] Child Support Recovery Act of 1992 as amended by the Deadbeat Parents Punishment Act of 1998 (18 U.S.C. § 228.)

You may feel strongly that your job as custodial parent includes ensuring that support obligations are met. After all, your child's welfare is jeopardized when support payments are insufficient, chronically late, or missing altogether. Although you should pursue legal enforcement of the support order, remember that *you are not the enforcer*. That is not to say that you should just stand by and watch the arrearages increase.

Non-payment of support is a very serious problem, so pursue legal channels to get those child support dollars flowing again. Make detailed notes in your parenting journal of missed payments, insufficient payments, or NSF checks when you get support payments directly from the other parent (and not through the Arizona Support Payment Clearinghouse). Then promptly contact your attorney for court enforcement action against the delinquent non-custodial parent.

Will Spousal Maintenance Be Awarded in Your Divorce?

In a divorce or legal separation, the court may order one spouse to provide financial support for the other spouse. Some states refer to spousal support as *alimony*, but in

Arizona it is known as *spousal maintenance* and it isn't just for women.

Spousal maintenance is an issue to be negotiated in every divorce. But unlike child support, there are no spousal support guidelines or statutory formulas to calculate the amount to be paid. Without guidelines and with the broad discretion the courts have in determining the amount and duration of spousal maintenance, such awards lack the uniformity and predictability found with child support orders.

As you might expect, with no guidelines to help predict one's financial future, the parties are often fearful about paying too much or not getting paid enough. There are statutory provisions that the courts must follow, however, so that is where I will begin this discussion.

Who Is Eligible for Spousal Maintenance?

With the exception of a covenant marriage, Arizona courts cannot consider any acts of marital misconduct when deciding whether to award spousal maintenance. And if you were wondering, which spouse initiated the divorce has no bearing on the court's decision either. When a party requests spousal support (and either may do so), records of past earnings, work history, personal income, medical disability, and educational background must be provided to substantiate the need for the maintenance sought. To determine the appropriateness of a spousal maintenance award, the court conducts a two-step analysis. [9]

Step One: Eligibility for Spousal Maintenance

As a threshold question, the party seeking a maintenance order against the other party must first establish eligibility for spousal support. Whether you ask the court to award maintenance or the other party wants support from you, be prepared for questions like the following in this initial award-determining step:

- Does the spouse seeking maintenance have sufficient property?
- What property will be apportioned to that spouse in the divorce?
- Is the spouse self-sufficient without additional financial help?
- Does the spouse need to stay home to care for a child?
- Is this spouse able to earn enough to become reasonably self-sufficient?
- Did the marriage last many years?

---

[9] A.R.S. § 25-319. Maintenance; computation factors.

- Will the spouse's age make self-sufficiency through employment impossible?

Depending upon the court's findings on these questions, it may order spousal maintenance for the party needing financial assistance. One likely candidate for support, for example, would be a 55-year-old stay-at-home parent with little education and minimal assets, who was married for 25 years, and who worked only occasionally while the other spouse was the primary wage-earner for the family. Another candidate for spousal maintenance might be a 26-year-old well-educated parent whose earnings are limited because he or she is custodian of a very young child or one who has special needs.

Whatever the unique circumstances may be, when maintenance is needed because the spouse cannot provide for his or her own reasonable needs, the court will continue on and determine an appropriate amount and duration for such support.

Step Two: Computation of Spousal Maintenance

In the second step – *deciding an amount and duration for an award* – the court considers all factors in the divorce that are relevant to spousal support. Even though judges have broad discretion in awarding maintenance, 13 factors provide a statutory framework for the court's analysis. In that computation process, you should anticipate providing evidence in answer to questions like the following:

1. **What standard of living was established during the marriage?** Was this an affluent family? Did they enjoy stylish society and maintain a high standard of living? Did the couple live modestly, getting by with limited resources?

2. **How long did the marriage last?** Was this a marriage of short duration, lasting only a year or two? Did the marriage last for a decade or longer?

3. **What is the age, earning ability, job history, emotional health, and physical condition of the spouse seeking support?** Was the spouse a stay-at-home parent raising the couple's children? What jobs has the party held? How much money could he or she reasonably earn in today's job market? Is the party well-educated? Would training or additional schooling realistically improve employment opportunities?

4. **Is the other party able to meet his or her own financial needs while supporting the other spouse?** How much does the supporting spouse earn? Is he or she retired or on a fixed income?

5. **How much can each spouse earn in the labor market and what financial resources are available to each of them?** Will one spouse substantially out-earn the other under most circumstances? Does one party have more assets than the other, so there is a financial imbalance between the spouses?

6. **How did the spouse seeking support contribute to the other's earning ability and career?** Did one party maintain the household and care for the children, freeing the other to concentrate on employment opportunities and career advancement?

7. **Did the spouse seeking support lose out on employment opportunities in benefiting the other's career?** Did one spouse put his or her education or employment goals on hold so that the other party could get ahead financially?

8. **Once the divorce is final, how will the parties contribute to their children's educational expenses?** Will a parent be able to assist with his or her child's educational costs only if spousal maintenance is received?

9. **What financial resources and property will be available to the party seeking support?** Does the spouse have sufficient property to take care of all reasonable needs without financial help? What property will make up that spouse's community assets?

10. **How much time is needed for the party seeking support to train and study for appropriate employment?** Could this spouse take vocational, college, or university courses to build a sustainable career? How much would it cost to get the education or training necessary to become financially independent?

11. **Did the spouse hide property and assets or commit other destructive or wasteful acts?** Although marital misconduct is not a reason to order or deny maintenance, the court may consider any excessive or abnormal expenditures and the concealment of assets.

12. **How will the spouses' health care insurance costs compare after the divorce is final?** What will the cost of coverage be for the spouse seeking support? Will the other party save money by converting family health insurance to his or her employer's insurance plan?

13. **Did either party abuse the other spouse or a child?** Did actual damages and judgments result from acts of domestic violence? Were there any criminal convictions for acts committed against the other spouse or child?

After considering all of the relevant factors, the court will decide how much money one spouse will be ordered to pay the other and for how long.

Not knowing with certainty how the court will decide the issue of spousal maintenance is often sufficient motivation for couples to try working out an agreement on their own, with the help of their attorneys. Once an agreement on spousal support is successfully negotiated (or mediated with the help of a professional mediator), the terms and conditions are included in the parties' separation agreement.

3 Tips for Negotiating a Reasonable Spousal Maintenance Agreement

Here are three tips to help guide you toward negotiating a reasonable spousal maintenance award during your divorce:

1. Line Up Your Experts

Particularly with marriages of long duration, look to financial experts for testimony on the earning potential and future financial resources of both spouses.

Vocational Evaluation: The employability and earning potential of the party seeking spousal maintenance is often a question for expert analysis. The professional services of a vocational evaluator may be very useful in supporting either party's position on what is a reasonable maintenance award. Vocational evaluators project the recipient spouse's potential earning ability. A report from the evaluator is also useful whenever there is possible under-employment (whether unintentional or deliberately contrived to receive more support or pay less support). When a party is under-employed and could be earning more in his or her field, then the vocational expert's report will reflect that.

Financial Evaluation: Not every spouse will be eligible for maintenance under Arizona law. When a spouse is eligible for maintenance, the other party may argue that support should be minimal because the other spouse already has sufficient means to provide for his or her own reasonable financial needs.

When expert testimony is needed, Certified Public Accountants and financial planners can offer projections on each party's resources. They predict the value and return on all manner of investments, report on tax-related issues, viability of income property, potential conversion of assets into income-generating properties, and so on. The conclusions accurately report the money needed to continue the standard of living enjoyed by the couple during the marriage. Maintaining a standard of living would include, for example, the replacement cost of any insurance coverage lost when the marriage is dissolved.

2. Make Use of Mediation

With private mediation, any issue may be presented for resolution including spousal maintenance. The parties retain control over the outcome by resolving issues like spousal support through mediation without turning to the court for a final decision. When resolved issues are written into a mediation agreement and signed by the parties, a consent decree will follow.

This may seem counter-intuitive, but mediation can represent a significant cost-savings for the parties. The fewer issues in dispute, the fewer issues to be litigated by the attorneys. In my experience, disputes over spousal support can be difficult to negotiate and time-consuming to resolve. Should a settlement be reached through mediation, at least one significant issue will be removed from the trial agenda.

3. Be Prepared for Temporary Orders

Either party may request temporary spousal support before trial. Because there are no court orders in place, problems regarding contributions from the other spouse to household expenses, among other things, tend to surface fairly quickly. If necessary, a spouse may request temporary court-ordered relief for the interim period, before any trial is even scheduled. The temporary orders govern the spouses' actions during the divorce proceedings and may address spousal support, access to personal items, and many other aspects of the family law case.

Motioning for temporary maintenance often initiates more serious negotiations between the parties. When the court is likely to order interim spousal support, the amount set temporarily may influence the court when it sets a permanent maintenance award. When interim orders are not requested, the party asked to pay support may argue that it is not needed – using the absence of temporary support as evidence that permanent support isn't needed either.

Starting, Stopping, and Modifying Spousal Maintenance

The court's spousal maintenance order will include the amount of support, how often payments are to be made (as a lump sum, monthly, annually, or other schedule), when the payments are to start and stop, and whether the award can be modified. Depending upon the parties' agreement, conditions controlling payment, amounts, and the termination of support are often included (for example, the termination of rehabilitative support if the recipient drops out of college).

If you and your spouse do not expressly agree to some other termination event and the decree is silent on the issue, then spousal maintenance terminates on the death of either party or upon the remarriage of the recipient.

Unless the final decree states otherwise, spousal support orders may be modified or terminated after the divorce is final on "a showing of changed circumstances that are substantial and continuing." If, following negotiations or mediation, the parties stated in their separation agreement that spousal support cannot be modified, then the court's final decree will reflect that restriction.

Chapter 4

PROPERTY:
Who Gets What and Why?

In the previous chapter, I discussed two very important financial matters in divorce: child support and spousal maintenance. There is yet another significant financial matter to address – the division of property in your divorce. Because there are so many aspects to discuss regarding the division of marital assets and debts, I have dedicated this entire chapter to the subject. You will read about property types, negotiating a property settlement, valuating assets, and dividing retirement accounts, personal property, virtual assets, business interests, real property, and much more. We will start with the fundamentals of who gets what property and why.

For anyone considering divorce, understanding how marital assets and debts will be divided is essential to a fair and equitable result. With your Arizona divorce, all marital property must be equally divided between you and your spouse. Property divisions have long-range consequences that affect a party's financial future, as well as the future of the children of divorce.

Arizona is one of only nine community property states (the others being California, Idaho, Louisiana, Nevada, New Mexico, Texas, Washington, and Wisconsin). As such, there are two important concepts to be mindful of as you prepare for your Arizona divorce. First, there is a presumption that all assets and debts acquired during the marriage belong to the community. Each spouse owns an undivided one-half interest in the marital assets and shares equal responsibility for marital debts. Unless there is a reason for an unequal division – such as a separation agreement with different terms – the court will divide community property equally between the parties. Second, the family law judge has broad discretion over the final division and distribution of community assets and debts. With that in mind, most parties negotiate their property allocation to avoid court intervention, arriving at a voluntary settlement to be included in their separation agreement.

You need to prepare yourself for the division of property in your divorce, starting with an understanding of who gets what and why.

Characterize Assets as Community or Separate Property

One of the first questions a client will ask me is "What can I keep in the divorce?" In Arizona, all property owned by the parties will be categorized as either *separate property* or *community property*. Separate property belongs to only one spouse and is not subject to division in a divorce. Therefore, identifying separate assets and debts is the first step in determining what each party has the right to keep. (Although the parties can always agree otherwise, as you will read below.)

Community property is the couple's marital property and it is most definitely subject to division in a divorce. Community property includes all things acquired during the marriage, regardless of whether an asset is held in only one spouse's name or both. The general presumption is that all assets acquired during the marriage belong to the community. There are a few exceptions to learn, however, before you begin categorizing your assets and debts as "S" for separate or "C" for community.

The exceptions to the general presumption are limited to instances where the asset was either owned before the marriage took place, or was acquired by gift or inheritance during the marriage. If a spouse received gifts and keepsakes during the marriage, those are that spouse's separate property and not subject to division in the divorce. If a spouse inherited a Prescott cabin in the pines during the marriage, for example, then the cabin is that spouse's sole and separate property – the other party has no marital interest in it.

Make sure that your parents understand that any gift of money or property that you receive before the divorce is final will remain your sole and separate property. And also that any inheritance you receive by Last Will and Testament or intestate succession during the marriage will also remain your sole and separate property and will not be divided in a divorce.

When Separate Assets Become Community Property

An asset that starts out as separate property, however, may lose its character as the sole property of one spouse and become the marital property of both spouses. Everything depends upon how the party used the separate asset during the marriage.

When either spouse commingles separate property with marital property, the separate property can transform into a marital asset – this is known as *transmutation*. The transmutation of property occurs by agreement between the spouses, by gift from one spouse to the other during the marriage, or by commingling separate property with marital property to the extent it is no longer distinguishable.

Most property divisions will involve some transmuted property, especially if the marriage was one of long duration or one in which many acquisitions were made. Do not be surprised, then, if some transmuted property is part of your divorce.

When and How Was the Asset Acquired?

In general, establishing the character of an asset as either separate or community is determined by the circumstances surrounding that asset's acquisition. That designation is not altered because of a subsequent marriage – separate property acquired while unmarried remains separate property after marriage. When community funds are used to pay down a separate mortgage or used to make improvements on separate property, then the non-owning spouse is entitled to *reimbursement* for his or her share of community money spent on the other spouse's separate property.

What About Dividing Debts in Divorce?

For many couples, one spouse will have a Visa card and the other will have a MasterCard, or some other bank card arrangement, so that their spending seems more independent. When contemplating divorce, one of the first things a party wants to do is disavow any responsibility for the other spouse's credit card debts. Well, as with assets, community debts are divided between the spouses in the dissolution of marriage proceeding. And just as with assets, there are separate debts and community debts.

You may (or may not) be relieved to learn that a debt incurred prior to the marriage remains a separate debt and is not a shared marital obligation. That is also the case with debts incurred by one spouse *after the divorce action is initiated*, although there are exceptions. For the most part, though, any debts that arose during the marriage (and before the divorce petition is filed) will be allocated as community obligations and will be divided between the parties.

Spouses are always free to voluntarily agree to the designation of an asset or debt as the separate property of one spouse or the community property of both spouses – this is part of the negotiation of every divorce.

Why Should You Negotiate a Property Settlement?

Every Arizona divorce involves negotiation and settlement – the parties may freely designate *any* of their assets as community property or separate property. The family law judge can depart from the presumed 50/50 split of community assets and debts when the parties have a *separation agreement*[10] providing for an unequal division of their marital property. But when the separation agreement is silent on an issue, the judge will step in and make a final decision that binds the parties.

Negotiation, then, is a very important process in divorce. Both spouses should go into these negotiations with a positive attitude about reaching agreements and really give it their best efforts. The parties' agreements on matters of child custody, child support, spousal maintenance, and division of property make up the written separation agreement that will be included in the court's final decree of dissolution.

Attempting to settle marital property and debt issues without going to trial is a laudable goal for every couple. But when the parties are simply unable to agree on an issue, the dispute will continue on to trial. Litigation is a lengthy and

---

[10] A.R.S. § 25-317: Separation agreements.

expensive process, one which gives the court authority to decide all outstanding issues, including how the property will be divided. For that reason alone, most parties to a divorce will settle.

Negotiating a property settlement is not a walk in the park; most spouses may want to schedule a series of short sessions, meeting in neutral territory, to get through every issue they need to address. The process of listing everything, placing a value on each item, and planning how each asset or debt will be divided takes time and cooperative effort. Some parties can sit at the kitchen table and work through a reasonable and equitable property division, while other couples cannot communicate with each other on any level.

In my experience as an Arizona divorce attorney, though, the task of dividing marital property becomes much more burdensome when the parties rely (and pay) their lawyers to do the dividing for them. Therefore, the parties should try reaching an agreement on the division of property as soon as possible – the sooner an agreement is reached, the less money will be spent on attorney's fees. Negotiating the future of the marital home is a good place to begin.

Who Should Move Out and Who Should Stay?

Negotiating to get the results you want takes some strategizing. When your spouse really wants you to do something, *you* have negotiating leverage. If your spouse really wants you to stay in the marriage, for example, then you may consider leaving the home before you begin negotiations. In doing so, he or she will then be motivated to negotiate in an effort to bring you back. If you stay and try to negotiate, then you may find yourself in a weakened position because your spouse wants you to stay and has little incentive to agree to anything other than the status quo. In the alternative, if your spouse really wants you to leave, then begin negotiating immediately while you are still in the home and refuse to leave until the matter is settled.

This advice comes with one important caveat: *When there is a risk of domestic violence, do not take chances! Always put your safety and the safety of your children first, even if that means leaving the home when you really want to stay there.*

Valuating Community Assets and Debts

Only after each item of community property has been accurately valued will the judge divide it equally. That makes valuating assets an important phase of the property division in divorce. To get accurate values on your property, turn to these professionals – property appraisers, real estate agents, CPAs, business valuators, and forensic accountants.

Valuating Real Estate

For an estimate on the market value of real estate, consider hiring a *certified general appraiser* for commercial and all other types of real property. A *certified residential appraiser* may be used if the subject property involves residential real estate. An Arizona licensed real estate appraiser will prepare a written report of the property, including potential uses, comparable properties in the vicinity, construction methods and materials used, and so on.

You should also consider seeking the opinion of licensed *real estate agents* – they know their turf and can offer detailed information about the market areas they serve. An experienced agent will provide useful information about other properties for sale in the area, the average listing period up to point of sale, and the average selling price.

Valuating Personal Property

Personal property *appraisers* of furniture, antiques, art, guns, china, glassware, jewelry, and the like, are frequently affiliated with auction houses and antique stores. In this profession, experience is essential to a proper estimate of value. Depending upon the type of personal property, more than one appraiser's expertise may be needed to get a complete valuation of all the items.

An emerging group of intangible assets have entered onto the divorce scene, offering unique valuation challenges. They are online virtual goods, services, and real estate found in gaming and in virtual 3D worlds like Second Life. If you find evidence of virtual currency purchases – including *Facebook Credits*, *Playfish Cash*, *Linden Dollars*, or *Microsoft Points* – when reviewing the other party's transaction records, there may be a need for an appraisal of the virtual assets, too.

Valuating Businesses

If a community asset includes one or more business enterprises, then make use of a valuation report prepared by a *business valuator* or *forensic accountant.* These professional business valuators are certified public accountants (CPAs) licensed by the state. The business valuator investigates the enterprise's financial operations by interviewing key personnel and by analyzing business records. After completing an investigation, the valuator prepares a summary report with an estimated value for the business.

How property is divided in divorce will have far-reaching financial consequences for both parties, so be diligent in locating and valuating the community interests. In some instances, it may even be necessary to hire a *private investigator* to locate and identify marital assets that have been concealed by the other spouse to avoid division.

How Are Retirement Accounts Divided?

In Arizona, wages earned during the marriage are considered property of the community. Similarly, deferred compensation benefits derived from employment during the marriage (pensions, 401(k)s, IRAs) are also marital assets subject to division in a divorce. The pension plan does not need to be vested for it to be community property. If the participating spouse has a traditional defined benefit plan, then an actuary is used to establish retirement age and life expectancy. If the participating spouse has a profit sharing plan, 401k, or IRA, then the value of the plan is based on its current balance.

If both spouses have separate retirement accounts, then both accounts will be divided. (The parties may agree to keep their respective retirement accounts intact, as part of their separation agreement.) As with any other acquisition, if the pension was completely funded or earned prior to the marriage, then the plan is the separate property of the participant spouse and is not subject to division in divorce.

When valuating and dividing qualified pensions and retirement accounts, be mindful that pensions and retirement benefits often combine separate and community property interests. (As when employment began before the marriage and continued into the marriage.) One method of calculating the community share is to take the number of months that the participant-spouse was married while under the pension plan, and divide that figure by the total months of participation in the plan. The resulting percentage is used to calculate the community portion of the plan, which is then divided equally between the spouses.

The pension plan administrator will not divide any pension without a Qualified Domestic Relations Order (QDRO). So try to have the QDRO prepared early and submit it at the same time as the final decree for the court's signature. The QDRO may be included in the property settlement, incorporated into the court's decree, or issued as a separate order.

The final decree of divorce will establish the parties' interest in the respective pensions, but the QDRO – the court's order to the plan administrator – is necessary to carry out that division. With the exception of the non-qualified plan, such as an annuity (which doesn't require a QDRO), the QDRO is filed with the pension plan administrator who implements distribution to both parties when it is time to start releasing pension funds.

I recommend that you hire an experienced QDRO attorney – a legal specialist in the field. The QDRO is a very specific and often complex court order splitting the retirement account as part of the asset division in divorce.

The court's QDRO accomplishes two things. First, it assures the required payment is made to the "alternate payee," preventing the employee-participant from disposing of that share in violation of the divorce decree. Second, the QDRO ensures that each party receiving a portion of the pension is responsible for a corresponding share of the tax liability.

What Happens When a Spouse Hides Assets?

Although it is unwise and can seriously undermine a party's case when discovered, many a divorcing spouse will attempt to hide assets from division. *When one party deliberately hides assets, direct action must be taken to bring those assets before the court for division.* All too frequently, a party will try to conceal property before the petition for dissolution is filed, in anticipation of divorce. So the more time a spouse has before the divorce petition is filed, the more likely the concealment of assets will occur. You should be on the lookout for possible concealment in your divorce (and if you are thinking about hiding assets, well, think again).

Finding Decoys?

If hidden assets are found too easily, then they could be a mere decoy for the greater treasure hidden more carefully. Many a divorce attorney has observed a party (sometimes their own client) using a decoy to divert attention from the more valuable concealed asset. Say, for example, that the decoy is a Phoenix bank account opened by one spouse and funded with marital assets, but not a lot of money when compared to the couple's resources. The account is easily discovered by the other party who, having found the treasure, stops looking for more clues. Meanwhile, the well-hidden asset is a large offshore bank account held under a different name. If the other party stops looking for clues, then it is unlikely that he or she will locate the concealed offshore account.

What Clues Are There to Finding Hidden Assets?

As part of the financial disclosures required in every divorce, both parties must complete discovery and list all of their assets and debts. When there is any suspicion that a spouse may be hiding assets, then the sleuthing must begin. What follows are four tips on where and how to search for clues to hidden assets in financial records.

Tip#1: Search for Clues in Tax Returns

Closely examine income tax returns for the last five years. Study the interest income schedules in the tax returns. When comparing the itemized accounts listed on the tax return with the accounts listed by the spouse, do they match up? Compare the real estate taxes and mortgage interest in the tax returns with the real estate details provided by the spouse, are they the same? Determine whether there was any overpayment of taxes which must be refunded to the taxpayer, possibly after the divorce is finalized – will there be a tax refund?

Tip #2: Search for Clues in Bank and Investment Accounts

Obtain copies of all bank, credit card, and investment account statements going back five years. Examine each statement carefully and look for any large transfers or withdrawals. A pattern of regular transfers of small amounts may also indicate concealment, so do not ignore those simply because they are recurring. How much and how often was money transferred? Where and for what purpose was the money spent?

A spouse may try to hide cash and, on some occasions, may use the pretense of a debt when none really exists. He or she may transfer money to a friend or family member for the purpose of collecting it later on, after the divorce. Was a payment made to a friend or family member on a so-called debt?

Look for any custodial account statements in the names of your child or stepchild. A custodial account could be used as a mere repository for a party to make deposits, with plans to recover the money after the divorce. Is there a custodial account that you were previously unaware of?

Pay very close attention to ATM withdrawals. Do the withdrawals reflect normal spending patterns? What was the money used for?

When reviewing credit card statements, look for payments for accommodations and travel expenses. Are there charges for housing expenses outside the marital home, such as rental payments? Is there any charge that was extraordinary or unusual?

Tip #3: Search for Clues in Paychecks

Request payment records from the party's employer and carefully examine paychecks for any deferred bonuses, options, or wages. What if earnings are deferred until after the divorce, but the wages were earned during the marriage? Any such delays in paying what is owed could be evidence of collusion between the employer and the employee-spouse. A payment deferred until after the divorce would appear to be that party's separate property, unless it is traced back to the community as earned during the marriage. Is the employer holding back any earnings or bonuses to be paid after the divorce? Is a promotion or a pay raise being stalled until after the divorce?

When a spouse is paid in cash, or partly in cash, tracking earnings may be much more difficult. Look for changes in the pattern of earnings established during the marriage. Is the spouse working the same number of hours, but with a significant reduction in stated earnings?

When a spouse has cash income, one way to establish whether there are hidden assets is to perform a *lifestyle audit*. The lifestyle audit involves comparing the party's stated income to the amount of money he or she actually spends. If the party's expenditures are unreasonably high given the stated earnings, then it may be evidence that assets have been concealed. Are the spouse's spending habits excessive when compared to the stated earnings?

Tip #4: Search for Clues in Business Records

Owning a business may make it easier for a divorcing spouse to hide assets. Sometimes hiring a business evaluator or forensic accountant may be necessary to thoroughly investigate the business records for possible concealment practices.

Wages may have been paid to family members or friends for work they did not actually perform – with the intent to return the money to the concealing spouse after the divorce is over. Were wages paid to family members or friends for work they did not do?

Investments can be written off as business expenses, too, and expenses can be inflated to reduce income. Is the business being restrained to look less profitable? Was business equipment purchased for much more than market value? Are the business expenses excessive when compared to the actual cost of operation?

Divorce for most couples is challenging enough without one party's attempts to hide assets from the other spouse. When concealment of assets is suspected, gather and photocopy all financial records before a petition for dissolution is filed. And if you haven't yet separated, consider safe-keeping those records in a secure location outside the home where they can be retrieved later.

How Does Marital Waste Affect Property Division?

The last topic I will discuss in this chapter is about recovering wasted marital assets. The party who committed marital waste will have to return one-half the amount wasted to the other spouse.

When community assets are dissipated to the detriment of the marriage, the possibility of marital waste needs to be carefully examined. Community property that was unjustly used by one party may be recovered by the other spouse in the divorce.

Here are some questions that must be answered when there was possible waste:

- *Did the spouse's spending deplete the marital resources?*
- *Did the marriage benefit from the spouse's spending?*
- *Did the spouse spend money on things unrelated to the marriage?*
- *Was the spouse's spending excessive given the couple's spending habits and the lifestyle they enjoyed during the marriage?*
- *Was the spouse spending money to acquire, divert, or hide assets?*
- *Was the spouse's spending extraordinary in any way?*

A party is free to dispose of his or her separate property in any legal manner, whether prudent or imprudent. But when assets are held by the community, one spouse cannot tap into and deplete the marital asset pool without consequences.

The waste of marital property can involve all kinds of activities including:

- Gifts and money spent to support an extramarital affair
- Frivolous, unjustified, or fraudulent spending

- Excessive withdrawals from financial and investment accounts, with no accounting
- Money spent to support excessive alcohol consumption or addiction
- Gambling losses
- Illegal activities like narcotic use
- Excessive gifting to the spouse's children from a previous marriage or to other family members
- Fault-based loss by foreclosure of the marital home
- Loss or damage to marital property
- Legal fees and property loss to forfeiture caused by the spouse's criminal activities
- Loss to business interests

When property is allocated during the divorce, the court looks into excessive, abnormal expenditures and examines any destruction and concealment of marital assets. Any indication that there was a fraudulent transfer or fraudulent disposition of community property will be scrutinized, too.

The burden is on the injured spouse to present sufficient evidence to support the court's finding of marital waste. Once evidence is presented, the other party has the burden of proving there was no waste (that is, proving that the asset was used to benefit the community or that there was no excessive or extraordinary spending).

Once it is proven that a marital asset was wasted by one spouse, the amount wasted is deducted from the responsible party's 50% share of the community property. But when the community assets are insufficient to compensate the injured spouse for the loss, the court may issue a money judgment against the responsible party for the balance still owing after the divorce is final. In that situation, the injured spouse becomes a judgment creditor and can continue collection on the debt according to law, including garnishment, until the debt is satisfied.

Chapter 5

PRIVACY AND SECURITY:
Why Should You Take Action?

In the first chapter of *The Arizona Divorce Handbook*, I mentioned the importance of taking precautionary measures to protect one's privacy and security before, during, and after the divorce. (See Chapter 1 for changing passwords and passcodes, and setting up a secure email account for privileged attorney communications.) This chapter covers the risks and repercussions associated with social media networking. Learn what a party should and should not do, especially when there are child custody matters to resolve in the case. I discuss certain legal restraints on what a party can lawfully do when seeking information from the other spouse – that is, crimes for spying, stalking, or harassing the other spouse. And lastly, I provide some guidance on getting restraining orders when domestic violence enters into the divorce.

What Is the Role of Social Media in Divorce?

Not too long ago, collecting damaging evidence against a spouse required hiring a private investigator. The PI would follow the target-spouse around for days or even weeks, staking out places, interviewing locals, snapping photographs, and collecting any proof of bad behavior. Hiring a PI to collect evidence is still useful in certain circumstances, but it is time-consuming and expensive. Not to mention out of reach for many who do not have sufficient means to pay the hourly rate and daily expenses of a private sleuth.

Today, a fair amount of the work is done voluntarily by the very spouse being investigated! One admission after another is posted on social media websites every minute, of every hour, of every day. People just do not exercise discretion when it comes to posting the details of their daily lives online. If Wife's lawyer wants to know where Husband has been spending his weekends, for example, a little Googling and a Facebook search is likely to yield recent results that can be useful in court.

Posting pictures and personal information about yourself on a public forum like Facebook is an open invitation for opposing counsel to collect evidence against you. Not only will the evidence be useful in the initial divorce, it is useful in any family law case including child custody, visitation, and support.

Using social media to network and stay connected with family, friends, and associates can be great so long as the user is cognizant of the risks associated with social networking via the internet. This should be the mantra for every party to a divorce: ***Anything you post can be used against you in family law court!***

The party who uses social media websites must understand that content posted online may be introduced as evidence (it must be relevant to the case, of course). At a minimum, a spouse in the midst of divorce should be very cautious with the message being shared when using social media to communicate and network. Wild Las Vegas weekends, for instance, do not play well in child custody proceedings.

Posting online publishes information and, once published, it can be gathered lawfully and used against the party in court. This means that new and old posts alike can, and do, influence matters of child custody, parenting time and visitation, child support, spousal maintenance, and the division of marital assets and debts in divorce. In Arizona and elsewhere, photographs and messages posted on social networking sites are considered to be strong evidence in court. Even a spontaneous post, intended only to be humorous and entertaining, can undermine a party's case with very unpleasant consequences.

Social Media Is Bigger Than Facebook

With social media networking so commonplace, it is getting easier for divorce attorneys to collect damaging evidence against an opposing party. For evidentiary purposes, social media includes cell phone use, emails, online photographs, uploaded videos, posts, text messages, comments, blogs, microblogs, tweets, and the like. Opposing parties and their attorneys routinely look to Facebook, LinkedIn, Twitter, YouTube, MySpace, blogs, and other social media forums to gather evidence for use in court.

Posting anything online can affect one's reputation in the community and, once published, it may never go away. One spouse could gather evidence from social media to demonstrate that the other party is an "excessive spender," the "irresponsible parent," or the one who is "drug or alcohol dependent," and that only touches on what may be gleaned from a few well-chosen pictures.

Social media evidence might be a photograph of an intoxicated parent (establishing a lack of child supervision in a custody dispute). There may be images of luxury items like tropical vacations and expensive cars (establishing undeclared income or hidden assets when determining child support or alimony). There may be evidence that a party is LinkedIn at work (establishing earning capacity). There could be evidence of the party sunbathing poolside at a Las Vegas hotel during a supposed job interview (establishing failure to seek employment). All can be very damaging to a spouse's case.

Evidence gathered through social media may be used to refute testimony, too. When a party posts a message that contradicts a statement he or she made previously in the divorce, then the other spouse will exploit that post as evidence establishing a lack of credibility and propensity for untruthfulness.

In addition to maintaining a low online profile during the legal proceedings, here are some useful tips on managing social media to protect your privacy and reputation:

- Consider logging off entirely until the divorce is final or the family law case is resolved.
- Do not post photographs of, or boast about, big-ticket purchases and vacations.
- Think before you post. Consider the legal ramifications of publishing anything personal and exercise discretion on all social media sites.
- Exercise restraint in posting any photographs of yourself.

- Clean up your image, and your page. If someone else (a friend, your teenager) has detrimental photos on their webpage evidencing your questionable behavior and judgment, then do what you can to get those removed, too.

- When you want custody and claim to be the more responsible parent, make sure that your page reflects that – remove the "wild and crazy" photographs.

- Do not discuss, comment, or tweet about the divorce, the judge, the other party, or the attorneys.

- When you must post a message, carefully choose your words, say what is necessary and avoid expletives.

- Do not post anything that your child should not see.

- Do not disparage the other parent or write anything that would alienate him or her from your child.

- Enable privacy settings and set them high. Even when you have blocked your spouse, a well-meaning friend may forward your post. It could eventually end up with opposing counsel.

- Search for information on social networking websites about yourself to heighten awareness of online vulnerabilities that need to be shared with your divorce attorney.

Always be mindful that something posted online is published and may be impossible to retract. All it takes is for someone to post something about you – a co-worker, neighbor, family member, or best friend. Those you have friended can share your post and information with others. To undermine your position in the divorce, all opposing counsel needs is a compromising statement or photograph that establishes where you were, who you were with, or what you were doing.

Gathering Social Media Evidence Against the Other Party

Anything you post can be used against you in a family law court, but the reciprocal is also true. Evidence gathered by you may be used in court against your spouse. When you know the other party uses social media to network, inform your attorney. If you observe potentially useful online information about your spouse, then relay those findings, too. Your lawyer's use of that online evidence could have a significant impact on the divorce.

Negative social media evidence can weaken a spouse's position during divorce negotiations, as when the evidence is used to disparage character or prove that the spouse lied. Many people will settle – even when doing so is clearly to their disadvantage – rather than have the information presented as evidence at trial to a judge. Why? When a spouse makes a statement in the divorce and the other party presents social media evidence exposing the statement as a lie, the spouse not only loses credibility with the court (and child custody evaluator), but the exposure can result in personal and professional embarrassment and humiliation.

The information gathered about a party must be obtained lawfully to be admitted into evidence. When a party has reason to believe that relevant evidence requires the collection of information under a subpoena, then online activities beyond social networking can be gathered from the company providing the online service. This is possible with interactive gaming and other online entertainment providers. (In a recent divorce case, for example, a subpoena was used to gather information about a party's online gaming. Proof of online gaming was relevant to the case because the parent was supposed to be home-schooling the child, but was instead playing "World of Warcraft" for up to 10 hours in a session. The gaming evidence led to primary legal custody going to the other parent.)

Always be discrete in your online conduct and communications to avoid being negatively characterized in court. Better yet, stay offline until the divorce is final.

Can Internet Activities Be Harmful?

Every party to a divorce should guard against internet activities that could violate Arizona law and become dangerous, namely cyber-spying, cyber-stalking and cyber-harassment. "Cyber" refers to the use of computers to spy, stalk, or harass another person.

Someone spies to obtain information secretively, without permission from the person who holds that information. Spying is espionage, or clandestine surveillance. When computers or electronic devices are used to secretly obtain intelligence, the act is *cyber-spying*. No matter how naïve the party, no matter how innocent the motive, attempting to acquire evidence by spying or cyber-spying on the other spouse is a very bad idea.

In Arizona, a person may commit a Class 5 felony by intentionally intercepting another's communication, even when one of the parties to the telephone conversation or email communication happens to be the other spouse.[11] When one spouse eavesdrops on the other spouse by intercepting a wire or electronic communication without consent, then the unauthorized listening is spying. As tempting as it may be to acquire information for the divorce by eavesdropping on the other party's private emails or phone calls, intercepting another person's private conversations without permission is a crime.

Although a party may successfully persuade someone else to do the intercepting for him or her, that still does not

---

[11] A.R.S. § 13-3005: Interception of wire, electronic and oral communications; installation of pen register or trap and trace device; classification; exceptions.

give the party a defense to the crime. In fact, it is a felony to trick, or connive, a communication service provider into disclosing the content of someone else's electronic communication. The party's mere possession of a device that could be used to intercept an electronic or oral communication, with the intent to use it, can be a criminal act.

In your divorce, do not spy on the opposing party's computer or emails. Doing so may seriously hurt your case. If you suspect your spouse has access to your computer passwords, social media accounts, or email accounts, then immediately change those passwords and open a new secure email account that no one else can access.

Another criminal act is **cyber-stalking**, which occurs when the internet or some electronic means is used to stalk a person. **Cyber-harassment** involves using email, instant messaging, blogs, and so on, to torment and harass someone. These are serious criminal activities – the torment can be both annoying and alarming to victims who are harassed. In Arizona, cyber-stalking directed at a specific individual is a form of intentional criminal harassment and a Class 1 misdemeanor.[12] Such intentional harassment can involve any of the following acts committed by one spouse against the other:

---

[12] A.R.S. § 13-2921: Harassment; classification; definition.

- Anonymously or otherwise contacting, communicating, or causing a communication with the other spouse by verbal, electronic, mechanical, telegraphic, telephonic, or written means in a manner that harasses.

- Continuing to follow the other spouse in or about a public place for no legitimate purpose after being asked to desist.

- Repeatedly committing an act or acts that harass the other spouse.

- Surveils (or causes another person to surveil) the other spouse for no legitimate purpose.

- On more than one occasion, making a false report to a law enforcement, credit agency, or social service agency.

- Interfering with the delivery of any public or regulated utility to the other spouse.

Restraining orders (Order of Protection) are often sought in domestic violence cases in Arizona and elsewhere, but they may also be issued to protect a spouse from the other party's stalking, cyber-stalking and harassment. The victim-spouse can seek a restraining order from the court to stop the other party from harassing him or her. If the judge's *order of protection* or *injunction against harassment* is violated, then the defendant-spouse may be charged with a

Class 6 felony for ***aggravated harassment***. Repeated harassment can result in a Class 5 felony, which is more severely punished.[13]

When Domestic Violence Is Part of Divorce

If the opposing party is violent, or threatens violence, towards you or your children, then a restraining order is necessary to keep him or her away. Animals may also be protected under such judicial order.

A court's order of protection prevents the defendant-spouse from contacting the protected spouse, and any other protected person, at home or at work. Typically, the order of protection is granted *ex parte*.

This type of restraining order is available when there is an act of domestic violence or threat of domestic violence against a family member, and "family" is broadly interpreted. For an order of protection, a family or intimate relationship is necessary between the victim and the defendant. That family relationship includes a spouse, previous spouse, blood relative, someone who lives with or lived with the person, the

---

[13] A.R.S. § 13-2921.01: Aggravated harassment; classification; definition.

father or mother of the unborn child, and someone in a current or past romantic relationship with the person.

If, at any time, you or your child is a victim of domestic violence, then file a petition for an order of protection against the abusive spouse immediately with the court. When a domestic violence crime has occurred, supporting evidence, dates, and testimony about the violent event is necessary for the court to issue the order. In making a decision, the judge may ask the petitioner-spouse for information about:

- Whether the defendant should be ordered to stay away from the petitioner's workplace.
- Whether the defendant should be prohibited from possessing a firearm.
- Whether the defendant should be barred from the petitioner's home.
- Whether there are others who should also be included in the protective order as "protected parties."

The filing spouse must swear that the information he or she provided in the petition is true and then signs its. After the judge signs the order, the defendant-spouse must be properly served with both the petition and the order. Law enforcement will serve the defendant for free (as well as an injunction against harassment). For a fee, a private process server will carry out service. The protective order is effective for one year, and that year begins when the defendant is served.

The protected spouse, as well as any other protected persons, should keep the order on his or her person at all times. If the defendant-spouse, who has not yet been served, shows up where the protected person is, then the police should be called and presented with a copy of the restraining order when they arrive. The officer will then serve the order on the defendant-spouse. Should the defendant violate the order of protection after being served, then he or she has committed a crime and will be arrested. Importantly, even with an order of protection in effect, the protected spouse needs to take every safety precaution possible and prudent under the circumstances.

An order of protection requires that the defendant stay away and remain out of contact with the protected person. Although the order is valid for a year, it can be modified or quashed (dismissed) by the court. The defendant can be arrested for violating the protective order, even when the protected person initiated the contact. The court may also order that the defendant-spouse not possess, receive, or purchase firearms or ammunition, and can order surrender of those firearms to law enforcement upon service of the protective order.

What should you do? Keep a diary, journal, or log of events with dates and descriptions of any incidents relevant to your case involving potential or actual violence, threats of violence, stalking, cyber-stalking, and harassment. In detail, describe specific examples of your spouse's poor judgment, alcohol or drug abuse, violent behavior, or threats of violence. Take notes of the conversations you have with your spouse over the issues in the divorce. Also save copies of all emails or written exchanges with your spouse. But remember...

Never take chances with your safety or your child's safety.

If you are in danger, DIAL 911.

Chapter 6

CHOOSING AN ATTORNEY: What Should You Look For?

In Arizona, you are not required to hire an attorney to represent you in the divorce, so the first question you should ask yourself is whether you will hire an attorney or not. Understand that as soon as the petition for dissolution of marriage and responsive pleading are filed with the Clerk of the Superior Court, the spouses become "parties" to a legal action in which their respective interests are often in opposition.

Many couples may think they are better off saving money by simply sharing legal fees and hiring one attorney to represent the both of them. I offer a few words of caution against attempting to share one divorce attorney between the two of you. Not only would this violate the professional ethical standards required of the attorney who is only permitted to work with one party in a divorce, it would jeopardize one and possibly both spouse's legal rights and interests – there is a direct conflict of interest in such dual representation.

In some instances, one spouse may hire an attorney while the other spouse represents himself or herself *in propria persona*, or *pro se*. That does not present an ethical issue for the divorce attorney because the legal representation is limited to one spouse. Be mindful, however, that the attorney will be advocating on behalf of his or her client only and not the pro se party. In many instances, and depending upon the complexity of the circumstances, it may be best to hire a divorce attorney to take control and drive the case to conclusion.

If you are unsure whether to hire any attorney at all, then take a moment to investigate what is involved in the do-it-yourself divorce. You may find that this is something you could accomplish on your own if the requisite divorce resources were made available to you.

The ***Arizona Divorce & Custody Coach*** at *www.onlinedivorcecoach.com* (a division of SDS Law) is a one-stop complete do-it-yourself resource center with unlimited email access to an Arizona licensed divorce attorney who can you guide you through the entire process.

Many people prefer to do the legal work themselves for a variety of reasons, but it is no cure-all and does not work for everyone. When done correctly, the do-it-yourself divorce often represents a significant savings on attorneys' fees. If the pro se party is not fully prepared for every legal proceeding, then the do-it-yourself divorce can cause substantial legal problems (which may or may not be correctable) and cost even more later on in attorneys' fees over damage control.

Once the decision to hire a divorce attorney is made, the next task to be taken seriously is selecting the right person to represent you. Choosing your attorney may be one of the most important decisions you will ever make. Without question, you want the most favorable results possible for yourself and for your children. Of course you need to know how much you will be charged, but you should not base your hiring decision on legal fees alone.

The more selective you are in choosing a divorce attorney, the more confidence you will have in the representation and in the legal proceedings. (The last thing you need at this time is increased anxiety stemming from a lack confidence in your attorney and concern over the legal merits of your case!) Most importantly, then, you want to hire an experienced attorney, one who is capable of guiding you through the entire divorce process efficiently and expertly. So before you make that hiring decision, get candid answers to these eight essential questions:

1. Is your law practice focused exclusively on divorce and family law?

2. What attorney credentials do you bring to the representation?

3. Have you ever been sanctioned for an attorney ethics violation?

4. Will you be the attorney handling my divorce or will my case be handed off to another attorney with the firm?

5. How much will the legal representation cost?

6. Will I receive copies of every document in my case and will my calls be returned promptly?

7. How much experience do you have with complex high asset property divisions and finding hidden assets?

8. How much experience do you have with contested child custody matters?

This is a great opportunity to ask specific questions about your case and increase your knowledge about divorce. Don't be timid. Communicate any concerns you have regarding circumstances specific to your family situation. For example, if you have an older child with a disability, you might inquire about special needs child support and the possibility of adult child support. In your search, what you hope to find is a family law attorney who really listens to your concerns, who answers your questions, and who you can trust with the most important aspects of your personal life.

1. Is Your Law Practice Focused Exclusively on Divorce and Family Law?

There are three constants in family law – change, change, and change. Our courts continuously interpret and reinterpret the laws. Our legislatures stay busy passing new laws and amending existing ones. Our judges vary in how they apply the rules of court, rules of civil procedure, and rules of evidence in their courtrooms.

To navigate your way through this legal maze, you want a seasoned attorney in your area whose practice is focused exclusively on divorce and family law. By seasoned, I mean an attorney who has tried many divorce cases successfully. Someone who has worked with complex asset divisions and has handled contested custody matters. Someone who anticipates and strategizes with professional confidence built on years of experience.

At the Law Offices of Scott David Stewart, our attorneys limit their practice to a single area and our family law practice is exclusive to divorce, paternity, child custody and parenting time establishment and modifications. We have earned respect within the legal community for our outstanding trial skills, our extensive knowledge of complex asset and property divisions, and our diligent handling of child custody matters. Seek out the attorney and law firm in your community that is recognized for those same qualities and has a similarly stellar reputation.

2. What Attorney Credentials Do You Bring to the Representation?

Any attorney that you consider must be knowledgeable about Arizona's laws and the federal laws affecting your divorce – insurance laws, tax laws, domestic violence laws, child support laws, child custody laws, and so much more. Before you hire counsel, examine the profiles and credentials of the entire legal team at the law firm – from partners, to associates, to paralegals. A favorable outcome in your case may depend upon it!

For example, I am "AV Rated" by Martindale Hubbell and rated "superb" by AVVO; both of these organizations consider peer reviews in rating attorneys, among other factors such as authorship and publications. Furthermore, every attorney at the Law Offices of Scott David Stewart is dedicated to carrying out the law firm's mission and upholding the firm's reputation for excellence in the practice of divorce and family law. Everyone at the law firm is concerned with providing the best customer service possible. With a little online investigating into the firm's website and by simply asking the right questions, you can assure that the attorney and law firm you ultimately choose has the best credentials.

3. Have You Ever Been Sanctioned for an Attorney Ethics Violation?

Attorneys are held to high ethical standards with regard to the practice of law and to the customer service they provide to their clients. You need assurance that the moral character and legal competency of your attorney justifies your hiring decision. The State Bar of Arizona regulates all of its attorney members and, when necessary, disciplines those lawyers with sanctions intended to punish for acts of professional misconduct. A grievance filed against an attorney may lead to reprimand, probation, suspension, restitution, and disbarment – the revocation of an attorney's license to practice law in the state.

At the Law Offices of Scott David Stewart, practicing law with the utmost degree of ethics is at our firm's very core. We take great pride in our reputation for high professional ethical standards and successful, experienced, dedicated family law representation for our clients. Not one of our lawyers has ever been found in violation of an attorney ethics rule. If the attorney you interview or a member of that law firm has been disciplined by the state's bar association (or sanctioned in any other state), then you need to know about it before you decide to hire.

4. Will You Be the Attorney Handling My Divorce or Will My Case Be Handed Off to Another Attorney With the Firm?

You may find that at some law firms the attorney who meets with you at the initial consultation is not the one who will be representing you in court. You deserve better than to have your case assigned to the attorney with a light caseload that week! If you are interviewing one attorney, but will be represented by another at the same law firm, then take the additional time to interview the attorney who will actually be handling your case. Yes, you have taken up some of the firm's time with the first interview. But really, is it asking too much to simply meet with your prospective advocate before you sign a retainer agreement and pay a retainer fee?

At the Law Offices of Scott David Stewart, the attorney you meet at your initial interview, and with whom you enter into a signed retainer agreement, will indeed be the attorney representing you throughout your divorce. Each of our attorneys develops a core relationship of trust with their clients – a relationship that requires direct, open, and frequent communication between attorney and client. You should insist on meeting with *the* attorney who will actually represent and handle the divorce so you can assess whether the direct, open, and frequent communication necessary for a positive outcome is even possible.

4. How Much Will the Legal Representation Cost?

This is a hugely important question, so do not be shy about asking it. You definitely need to ask, point blank, how much you will be charged for lawyer services and what the retainer fee will be, if any. Managing legal expenses requires planning and budgeting. To budget properly you need to know when you will be billed, so ask what the attorney's billing practices are. Some lawyers do not send statements out to their clients for months at a time, which may result in a surprisingly large bill covering months of services that exceeds the funds you have available to pay.

Additionally, some attorneys will charge a premium rate for their court appearances. Make sure to ask how the lawyer's *time* will be billed when working on your divorce. Some law firms charge a minimum fee for any task, regardless of whether the work took the attorney two . minutes or 15. If the attorney charges $300 an hour, for example, a five-minute telephone call could cost you $75!

By contrast, if you meet with an attorney at the Law Offices of Scott David Stewart, a thorough discussion on the cost of legal representation *always* precedes any signed representation agreement. We want every client to make an informed decision and be completely comfortable with our law firm's fee structure. To accomplish this, we carefully explain our billing system so that, when payments are due, the client is never surprised with hidden expenses or unexpected legal fees. (And we charge for attorney time in 1/10th increments, so when the task takes five minutes the client is not charged for a quarter hour!) We explain any costs and fees necessarily required in the client's divorce. We discuss our payment options, so the client can stay in control of his or her legal expenses. Our invoices are sent out once a month which ensures that the client is aware of the work performed, how long the work took to complete, and what the cost was. At our firm, we do not charge higher rates for appearing in court on behalf of a client – our attorney rates always remain the same. That is precisely the kind of up-front cost disclosures you need to know before you hire a divorce attorney.

6. Will I Receive Copies of Every Document in My Case and Will My Calls Be Returned Promptly?

When you interview a prospective attorney, be certain to ask how the law firm assures that you will have access to all case documents whenever *you* need them. Nothing is more worrisome to clients than not knowing what has transpired in *their* divorce. Nothing is more frustrating for clients than being told to respond to pleadings that they have never seen and know nothing about.

Unfortunately, some attorneys fail to provide their clients with copies of filed court documents (like motions from either party), orders issued by the court, or correspondences between the attorneys. To make matters worse, some lawyers chronically fail to return their client's telephone calls within a reasonable time (that a client's call should be returned within 24 hours is a concept lost on some busy attorneys).

So you know what to look for, at the Law Offices of Scott David Stewart we make the best use of the most current technology to keep our clients fully engaged in their family law case. A client uses our secure portal to login and view all of his or her case documents. Access through the portal is available to the client 24/7 – that's meaningful assured access anytime from anywhere. Substantive and procedural information on almost every topic in family law is readily available to clients on our website – they can read up on any subject relevant to their case (or simply of interest to them) at any time, at no additional cost.

We also send the client copies of all divorce-related documents that either arrived at our office or left from our office. And if a client calls when the attorney or member of our team is not immediately available, then the call will be returned within 24 hours. That's the kind of outstanding customer service that our clients highly value and something you should look for in your attorney.

Does the attorney and law firm have adequate internal management systems in place to assure that you are always apprised of what is happening in your divorce? Will you be able to reach your attorney when you need to, without unreasonable delay? If the answers to these questions leave you with doubts, then look elsewhere for competent legal representation and responsible customer service.

7. How Much Experience Do You Have With Complex High Asset Property Divisions and Finding Hidden Assets?

The division of assets and debts in some divorces may be very complex and openly contentious, which can be challenging for the parties, their attorneys, and the court. Adding strain to an already emotionally tense situation, some individuals will attempt to conceal assets from the other spouse.

Not all divorce attorneys are knowledgeable about business valuations, stock portfolios, financing matters, tax and debt issues, or how to identify and successfully uncover hidden assets. Therefore, before you make the decision to hire a lawyer, you need to know whether that person is experienced in dealing with complex and high asset divorce cases. Does that attorney know how to search out clues to hidden assets?

If your spouse is suspected of deliberately concealing assets, then aggressive legal action must be taken by your lawyer to bring those assets before the court. You need an attorney and law firm that is vigilant, always on the lookout for clues in documents, as well as lifestyle indicators of more money spent than the party claims to earn.

Whenever property division and debt settlement is complicated by a party's concealment, the Law Offices of Scott David Stewart has the experience and financial tools necessary to ensure that the client is not taken advantage of financially in the divorce. We routinely work with forensic accountants and investigators to uncover secreted assets and undeclared property. That diligent attention to detail and focus on the client's best interests is precisely what you should look for when interviewing an attorney prospect.

8. How Much Experience Do You Have With Contested Child Custody Matters?

Lastly, when you have minor children it is essential that your attorney be experienced with contested child custody matters. Of course, not every divorce involves contested custody issues, but you want to hire the attorney who knows how to avoid problems without diminishing your legal position. Who will not inflame (intentionally or unintentionally) an already highly emotional situation to the detriment of your children's best interests. Who is prepared to advocate your position through litigation if you and your spouse cannot agree on custody.

In all child custody cases, whether part of a divorce or separately brought as a family law case, the dominate principle is that custody will be awarded to the parent who the court believes will act in "accordance with the best interests of the child." In Arizona, there is no legal presumption favoring one parent over the other. If you desire primary physical custody or sole legal custody, then search for the legal advocate with lots of child custody experience.

At the Law Offices of Scott David Stewart, we believe that child custody is best settled through voluntary agreement between the parents. We know from experience, however, that child custody cases are often protracted and may need to be intensely litigated. In other words, voluntary settlement is not always possible. Consequently, your divorce attorney must be very knowledgeable of custody matters and be prepared to take action necessary to help you get the best custody arrangement possible.

Whenever custody is part of divorce, there are a number of procedures and professionals involved to assist in determining what is in the child's best interests. Mediation, parenting conferences, child custody evaluations, and settlement conferences are all part of child custody determinations. The child may have legal advocates, too. A best interests attorney and child's attorney may be appointed to represent the minor throughout the court proceedings. Be sure to inquire – before you commit to a particular law firm – whether the divorce attorney you are considering has ample experience with all of these child custody procedures.

Meeting with a lawyer for the first time is a very big step. When you commit to hiring a divorce attorney, the whole idea of terminating the marriage solidifies – it is no longer a mere potential, it has become reality. That reality may seem overwhelmingly palpable for a while and strong emotions are to be expected, so don't be too tough on yourself. (Remember from Chapter 1 – when you need help dealing with the emotional aspects of your divorce, reach out and talk to a trusted friend, pastor, counselor, or family member.)

To help you through this transition, I'd like you to reflect on a few things as you begin working with your new divorce attorney:

First, be mindful that your attorney wants to help you move on with your life, the life that *you* imagine for yourself. Once you have explained your goals and objectives to your attorney, he or she knows what you need, want, and hope for. Your stated goals and objectives will influence your attorney at every step in the divorce process.

Second, bear in mind that your attorney is on your side, but there is no guarantee that you will get everything you want and hope for. Keep your expectations realistic, while preparing to challenge the other party on those issues most important to you. Your attorney will explain each phase of the divorce so that you understand what will be happening and how your rights and responsibilities will be affected. Whenever advocacy is needed, your attorney will be there to present your side within the confines of the family laws applicable to your divorce.

Third, be mindful that your attorney will be helping you through some very complicated issues, including the property settlement that is part and parcel of every divorce. Before you can even begin to negotiate a property settlement, your attorney will advise you on how property is divided. Once you understand your property rights and have allocated assets and debts as either community property or separate property, you can start moving toward a property settlement.

Fourth, keep in mind that your attorney will be drafting any separation agreement that you and your spouse have worked through, so the agreement becomes enforceable for both of you by becoming part of the court's final decree of dissolution.

Fifth, know that throughout the entire family law case, your attorney will be scheduling and calendaring every significant date and deadline. This ensures that every matter, every proceeding, goes as smoothly as possible and that documents, pleadings, and hearings occur on time as scheduled and without unnecessary delays. You will be given plenty of reminders of what you need to do and when you need to do it, as each important date approaches.

One final thought. This may be your first experience with divorce, but your lawyer has been through all of the procedures many times before. Rely on your attorney's advice and legal discernment and rest assured knowing that your legal advocate is working diligently on your behalf.

Chapter 7
LIFE AFTER DIVORCE:
Envision What Your New Life Will Be Like

This final chapter is all about you, your future, and the future you aspire to provide for your children. As is so often true in life, a good result begins with a good plan.

Standing at the courthouse steps with divorce papers in hand, recognize that you are not the same person you were when you married. Before traveling too far on the path to marital dissolution, reflect on what your life and lifestyle will be like after the divorce is finalized. You have grown and changed in many ways from the person who walked down the aisle so long ago. This is an opportunity to reinvent yourself, and only you know what dreams and aspirations are worth pursuing.

Moving on with a new life requires letting go of lingering hard feelings aimed at the other party. Hanging on to the baggage of angry thoughts and hurt feelings, blaming your spouse for what went wrong, will only sap your energy and waste your time. In my experience, the more blame and fault there is in a divorce, the more time it takes to resolve issues, the more the children will suffer, and the more money it costs the parties. Blame is toxic and will only hinder your ability to move forward with your goals and a new life. Do not let blame chain you to the past. Instead, keep your focus on the future and what you must do for yourself and for your children.

On the surface that sounds easy, but for some the idea of moving on *alone* can be overwhelming. If you are trapped in a painful emotional cycle and cannot break free from negative thoughts and feelings, then consider meeting with a divorce counselor. Together you can prepare for what lies ahead, step-by-step. In Chapter 1, I discussed the emotional issues often tied to divorce and stressed the importance of seeking help whenever you need it. You may want to review that chapter now.

Setting Goals for a Promising Future

You are committed to dissolving the marriage, but have you taken time to define important goals so you have some direction? Getting what you want from the divorce requires preparation and strategy. Where the parties are at after the divorce is final depends, in part, on what happens during the divorce process. Once you know what it is you want, then you can begin setting realistic goals to achieve those ends.

Listing Long-Term and Short-Term Goals

There are many financial implications to divorce, all of which require thoughtful consideration. Start asking yourself key questions and write down your thoughts and answers – these will become the goals that guide you through the divorce and thereafter. Ask yourself:

- What will you need right away?
- How do you want to live?
- How will you support yourself and your children?
- Do you want career employment?
- Where do you want to live when the divorce is final?
- What will your lifestyle be like when you are on your own again?
- What are your expectations for the distant future?
- When do you expect to retire?
- Will you send your children to college or university?

To stay on the path to *financial independence*, an employed spouse may plan for continuing education or the return to university for a degree. The spouse who has been unemployed for a lengthy period may plan on upgrading skills and searching for entry-level employment opportunities. Contemplate these questions:

- Will a job opportunity require relocation to another city or state?
- What is the cost of tuition and where will the money come from?
- Will spousal maintenance be needed? How much? For how long?
- Will student loans be necessary and, if so, how much of a financial burden can you carry when working in the chosen field?
- Will an obligation to pay spousal support delay business pursuits or employment objectives?

Establishing long-term and short-terms goals is an important, necessary step in the divorce process so take the task seriously and write your goals down on paper (not on concrete, so you can make changes later). Think of your long-term goals as the theme underscoring the vision you have for your future and your children's future. Your short-term goals should keep you on track with accomplishing those long-term objectives. For example, if your long-term goal is a career in physical therapy, then your short-term goals may include finishing the degree program and preparing for certification.

With a clear vision for the future, implementing strategies to achieve your goals will become much easier during the divorce and thereafter. Before you take a position on any issue in your case, always reflect on the goals you have set for yourself and stay focused on the outcome you desire.

Learn What the Law Requires of Both Parties

Success in achieving a desired outcome in divorce depends largely upon the party's legal rights and obligations under Arizona law. Yes, you need to be clear on your goals, but you also need to be realistic about those objectives. It would be unrealistic to ask the court for orders that are contrary to the law. Learn what is possible under the laws of this state and adjust your expectations to fit within those parameters.

For example, consider how the law deals with issues involving child custody and parenting time. One party may seek primary physical custody and ask to limit the other parent's visitation to one weekend a month during the school year. As reasonable as those expectations may be, they must be adjusted to account for the other parent's right to parenting time and for what is deemed to be in the child's best interests.

Freely Access Our Website as Your First Resource

I have been stressing the importance of getting a divorce education, but you may be wondering where to find reliable information once you have finished reading. I recommend that you visit my law firm's main educational website, which was designed specifically around Arizona divorce and child custody. Access is free! All of the legal information you need to get started in your divorce can be found at **www.sdsfamilylaw.com**.

When you envision your future and begin setting goals, do so with a firm understanding of what is legally possible under Arizona law. As you prepare for life after divorce, start thinking about making necessary changes to your insurance coverage and estate plan, too.

Changing Insurance Coverage

Getting a handle on finances after divorce also involves careful examination of insurance coverage. Whenever circumstances change significantly, as with a divorce, insured's should review certificates of insurance for automobile, homeowner's, life, and disability insurance coverage. Update insurers with your new contact information. If the other party is to pay the premiums and a payment is missed, for any reason, then you need to be notified immediately. Be sure to speak with an insurance agent about the risks and benefits associated with any changes to premiums, deductibles, or basic policy coverage before committing to those changes.

Minimum Automobile Insurance Coverage

Your insurance budget will have to cover a number of policies, including mandatory insurance for your personal vehicle. Premiums depend upon the make, model, year, and condition of the vehicle, the distances regularly driven, male or female, driving record, and credit history.

Under the *Fair Credit Reporting Act* (FCRA) insurance companies have a "permissible purpose" in examining a potential insured's credit information. When problems leading up to the divorce included financial issues between the spouses or bankruptcy, then negative credit information and a low credit score can result in higher premiums.

In Arizona, a *certificate of insurance* is necessary to register a vehicle and drive lawfully. The minimum automobile insurance coverage to operate a vehicle legally is bodily injury ($15,000 per person, $30,000 per accident) and property damage ($10,000 per accident).

For additional coverage above the required minimum, expect premiums to increase correspondingly. *Bodily injury coverage* pays for injuries the insured caused to others in an accident, but it does not pay for the insured's injuries (for that, add *medical payments coverage* to the policy). *Property damage coverage* pays for the damage the insured caused to other vehicles or property in an accident; it does not pay for damage to the insured's vehicle (for that, add *collision coverage* to the policy). For the insurance company to pay for damage or loss to the insured's vehicle because of theft, glass breakage, fire, violent weather, vandalism, hitting an animal, and so on, add *comprehensive coverage* to the policy.

Selecting Homeowner's Insurance

If there is a mortgage or deed of trust on your home, then you must have sufficient *property damage coverage* to satisfy the lender's minimum insurance requirements. When the home is totally destroyed, the borrower is still obligated to pay off the loan. Make certain that the homeowner's insurance policy sufficiently covers the debt should a destructive event occur, such as a fire.

Property damage coverage includes loss to the real property. *Contents insurance* covers loss to the personal property and possessions located at the home. When the homeowner has special collections, expensive jewelry, valuable antiques, or sophisticated computer equipment, for instance, then additional contents coverage should be scheduled to ensure adequate protection against the loss of these valuable items.

Personal liability insurance coverage protects the insured should someone be injured on the property as a result of homeowner negligence or for which the homeowner becomes legally responsible. The insurance company covers the defense costs up to the agreed upon limit stated in the policy.

If anyone tends to the landscaping or makes repairs to the home, then there is a risk that the worker may be injured and the homeowner could be held liable for damages. With *medical payments insurance* coverage, a person injured on the premises will have some or all medical expenses paid without regard to fault for the injury. This coverage does not extend to any intentional acts of the homeowner, however, and does not cover a renter, home business, the homeowner or family member residing there.

When comparing insurance premiums, be prepared to answer questions about your home's construction, the year it was built, the location of fire hydrants, and the distance to the nearest fire station, among other things. In Arizona's outlying areas, the nearest fire station may be many miles away which can result in higher premiums for rural homeowners.

What to Do About Life Insurance?

A life insurance policy pays out a specific amount of money to the beneficiary in the event of the insured's death. During the marriage, couples often have life insurance policies that name the "surviving spouse" as the primary beneficiary. Once the divorce is final, an immediate change in beneficiary designation may be in order. (Most insurers require the use of their official change of beneficiary designation form which is mailed or emailed to the insured upon request.)

As part of the divorce settlement, the party ordered to pay child support or spousal maintenance may also be required to maintain a life insurance policy to ensure that those support payments continue even after the death of the obligor. If you are the one receiving support, you may have concerns that the policy will lapse or that the beneficiary will be changed without your knowledge. If you have those concerns, consider arranging to pay the premiums on the life insurance policy yourself.

Term life insurance policies provide coverage for a specific length of time. There is no equity or cash value, so a term life policy is not an investment tool. As the insured gets older, the premium may increases or the pay-out on death can decrease. When it comes to cost savings, though, these policies are a useful option and easier on the insurance budget.

A *variable life insurance* policy is a combination of insurance and investment, and investments always involve risk. Once the money is taken out to pay the premium, the remainder is invested. For this policy to work as an investment vehicle, more money is paid by the policyholder than is needed to cover the insurance premiums. There is a guaranteed minimum payment on death under the insurance. There is a potential that the invested portion will also provide money on death, but as with any investment there is no guaranteed rate of return. These policies tend to be much more costly than other life insurance products.

A *whole life insurance* policy provides coverage over the course of the insured's lifetime at a set premium. Typically, the premium is paid over the duration of the policy, right up until the death of the insured. Unless the insured is willing to pay life insurance for life, other insurance products may be more useful and cost effective.

Why Disability Insurance Coverage?

Individual disability insurance will cover the insured's monthly income for a specific period if rendered unable to work because of illness or injury. For the party paying spousal maintenance or child support, a disability insurance policy can cover expenses if he or she becomes disabled and cannot earn an income. Many people fall into arrears on their support obligations because of illness or injury, so even a few months of disability coverage can make a big difference.

What About COBRA?

If one spouse is covered by the other spouse's employer insurance program, then the divorce is a "qualifying event" that gives the non-employee spouse COBRA coverage for up to three years (36 months). Although this may represent a cost-savings compared to independently acquired coverage, the premiums must still be paid or coverage will lapse.

With every insurance decision, carefully examine the level of risk you are comfortable with given your insurance budget. When discussing coverage with an insurance agent, get all of your questions answered before agreeing to a new policy or changing or terminating an existing policy.

Revising Estate Plans After Divorce

You will soon begin a new and independent chapter in your life, a chapter with new objectives and responsibilities. Because your legal status and financial circumstances are about to undergo a major transformation, take time to carefully review your estate plan. These are the kinds of instruments typically found in Arizona estate plans:

- *Last Will and Testament*
- *Letter of Instruction for Funeral and Burial*
- *Beneficiary Deed*
- *Durable General Power of Attorney*
- *Limited Power of Attorney*
- *Health Care Power of Attorney*
- *HIPPA Authorization*
- *Living Trust or Inter Vivos Trust*
- *Payable-on-Death Accounts or POD Accounts*
- *Life Insurance Policy*

Isolate those estate planning documents that need modification or revocation (termination). If you do not have an estate plan yet, then this is an excellent opportunity to begin conceptualizing one. You may wish to schedule a consultation with an estate planning attorney while the divorce is still pending. Although you can certainly *prepare* to revise your estate plan during the divorce, refrain from taking any action that might violate the preliminary injunction.

The most basic component of an estate plan is the *Last Will and Testament*. We should all periodically re-examine our Last Wills to ensure that they are still consistent with our testamentary intentions. Reviewing an estate plan every three to five years is good practice, but you should also review the plan when your circumstances have significantly changed – as with the birth of one's first child or the finalization of a divorce.

If you do not have a Last Will and do not survive the finalization of your divorce, then all of your assets may go to the "surviving spouse" under Arizona's laws of intestate succession.[14] The death of a spouse will terminate the divorce proceedings – it is the death that ends the marriage.

One or the Other – Testate or Intestate

When a person dies with a Last Will and Testament, he or she is said to have died *testate*. The enforceable terms

---

[14] A.R.S. § 14-2102: Intestate share of surviving spouse.

of the Last Will control the administration of the decedent's testate estate and the distribution to the devisees named therein.

By contrast, when a person dies without a Last Will, he or she is said to have died *intestate*. Arizona's laws of intestate succession apply to administration of the decedent's intestate estate and control the distribution of assets to the heirs at law. With intestate succession, Arizona law determines who the heirs are – that is, who will inherit from you and who will not.

If your Last Will was drafted after the marriage, then your spouse was probably named personal representative, or executor, as well as primary beneficiary of your estate. This is why reviewing estate documents early on, while the dissolution is pending, is important. Although some changes may be made without violating the preliminary injunction (as with a change in health care power of attorney and living will), you can have a completely revised estate plan prepared and ready for your signature as soon as the marital dissolution is finalized.

How to Reduce the Cost of Your Divorce

Every divorce involves unique circumstances and complexities, but in my experience there is one commonality – the need to keep attorney fees and legal expenses under control. As a wrap-up to this final chapter, here are six money-saving tips to help you keep the costs associated with your divorce at a minimum.

Tip #1: Start Your Divorce Education Today

I mentioned the importance of educating yourself on the family law issues that are relevant to your case. (Your decision to pick up a copy of this book was a great place to begin!) Just as with any new job, once you have a reasonable understanding of the task at hand, your efficiency will improve markedly – including an improved capacity to focus negotiations with your spouse and discussions with your attorney.

You are not preparing for certification as a paralegal, of course, but you do need to understand routine domestic relations issues. If you have children, then learn what is involved in child custody, parenting time, and child support. If you are a small business owner, then learn how the division of community assets and debts will affect your company's future. If you are a service member, then learn how military pensions are divided in divorce.

Consider setting aside an hour a day to study the general concepts of divorce, child custody, child support, spousal maintenance, and property division, familiarizing yourself with the legal terminology and procedures. As a result, you will grasp issues and strategies more quickly, with less explanation time needed from your attorney. You will also get more value out of those consultations and better engage with your attorney. The more knowledgeable you are about the issues in your divorce, the more informed your decisions will be.

Tip #:2 Avoid Litigation to Resolve Disputed Issues

Litigation is a very expensive method for resolving disputed issues in a divorce. So, if you really hope to save money, avoid litigation at every opportunity. And *never* attempt to use litigation as a way of punishing your spouse.

There are alternatives to litigation. Whenever possible, agreeing to alternative dispute resolution (ADR) methods like mediation can help resolve many issues, if not all of them. Once the list of issues is winnowed down to what simply cannot be resolved amicably through negotiation and

ADR, then those are the remaining matters to be litigated at trial.

Tip #3: When You Have Agreement, Write It Down

When you and your spouse come to an agreement on any issue, then write it down. Is there agreement on who will take which vehicle? Write it down. Is there agreement on who will stay in the marital home? Write it down. Every agreement represents one less issue to be resolved through negotiation, mediation, or litigation. You may actually find that you and your spouse are in agreement on a fair number of the major decisions that must be made.

Tip #4: Hire an Attorney With a Reasonable Fee Arrangement

I devoted Chapter 6 to choosing an attorney, so as a reminder look for a lawyer who tells you upfront what the fees will be. Attorneys are not clairvoyant, but they should anticipate the proceedings and how many attorney hours are likely to be involved at each step. The attorney's billable rate must be discussed at the initial consultation. So you can budget accordingly, you need to know how often the attorney bills, how much of a retainer fee is required, and whether different services have different rates.

What you definitely do not need is an attorney who routinely delays the case and drags the divorce process out. That approach will cost you more money and will add to your stress. You deserve nothing less than efficiency and proficiency from your divorce attorney.

Tip #5: Apply a Cost-Benefit Analysis to Every Issue

The adage "choose your battles wisely" has application in divorce. Not every issue is worth fighting over, so be practical and selective about what you want to spend your divorce dollars on. As challenging as it may be at times, do not allow emotions to interfere with rational thinking.

When you look at every issue from a cost-benefit perspective, you cannot help but stay focused on getting the divorce finished and done with. If you had to choose, would you prefer to pay your attorney to negotiate a used-microwave oven or spousal support? Which is really more important? This example may seem silly, but people do get caught up in their emotions and what they perceive to be a fairness issue. When it comes to negotiations, focus on the important issues and let the little things go by the wayside.

Tip #6: Do Much of the Basic Leg-Work Yourself

The time and effort you put forth toward being fully prepared will save you money. When your attorney asks for photocopies of all financial accounts, be thorough and provide complete copies. You want your attorney to be businesslike and efficient, you should be the same. Maximize your attorney's time and do not waste it. For example, you do not need to speak directly with your attorney (and pay the attorney hourly rate) when the legal assistant has the information for you.

No matter which member of your legal team is on the telephone with you, keep your conversations focused and to the point. When you have a conference scheduled with your attorney, be fully prepared for the issues to be discussed. When in negotiations, take reasonable positions (even when the other party does not). Always be mindful of the need to steer clear of litigation whenever possible. And never forget the old adage "time is money" – it is the attorney's time and your money that we are talking about.

By taking a practical approach to cost reduction at each stage in the divorce, you will enjoy significant savings over the entire process. A divorce can be quite economical, especially when the parties are cooperative with each other.

About the Author:
Scott David Stewart, Esq.

Author Scott David Stewart is an Arizona licensed attorney whose law practice focuses exclusively on family law and domestic relations. Mr. Stewart is AV Rated by Martindale Hubbell and rated "superb" by AVVO. He is a member in good standing with the State Bar of Arizona, Maricopa County Bar Association, and American Bar Association.

Early in his legal career, Mr. Stewart worked as a Deputy County Attorney in the Major Crimes Division of the Maricopa County Attorney's Office. As a felony prosecutor, Mr. Stewart successfully prosecuted thousands of serious felony crimes including domestic violence, aggravated assault, and vehicular and drug crimes. While at the County Attorney's Office, Mr. Stewart honed his trial skills and developed the strategies for success that he continuously implements in his law practice today.

The one haunting reality that Mr. Stewart observed first-hand as a prosecutor was the importance of passionate legal representation on behalf of those who, all too often, have little or no voice in the legal process affecting their lives. In divorce proceedings particularly, the children's voices and needs are often relegated behind the desires of their parents. Because of this, his primary goal has always been to ensure that children are the focal point of any dispute between parents.

In his early days, after graduating from Northern Arizona University with a Bachelor of Arts Degree in Speech Communication, Mr. Stewart attended the Illinois Institute of Technology, Chicago-Kent College of Law where he received his Juris Doctor. Chicago-Kent's outstanding reputation for producing trial attorneys, as well as their signature certificate program in Litigation and Alternative Dispute Resolution, made this renowned institution his law school of choice.

During law school, Mr. Stewart became a certified mediator with the Center for Conflict Resolution and successfully mediated high conflict landlord-tenant disputes for Chicago's Cook County Circuit Court. He participated in the law school's criminal defense clinic where, along with several other law students and their clinical professor, the author researched, investigated, and uncovered evidence proving a death row inmate's innocence. You may have seen Mr. Stewart profiled as a law student on the nationally syndicated television show **Extra**® and numerous other local media news stations.

The hands-on experience gained in law school taught the author those essential litigation, investigation, and negotiation skills that he now utilizes so persuasively in representing his family law clients.

Born and raised in Phoenix, Mr. Stewart is a first generation Phoenician with strong community ties to the *Valley of the Sun*. The son of a small business owner, Mr. Stewart gives much credit to his parents for helping him develop an entrepreneurial spirit and strong emphasis on core values such as integrity, respect, responsibility, leadership, work ethic, and family. These values guide the author daily in his representation of family law, divorce, and child custody clients.

As the founding attorney of the Law Offices of Scott David Stewart, pllc – an Arizona boutique family law firm with offices in Phoenix, Chandler, Scottsdale, and Peoria – Mr. Stewart's vision was to establish a unique law firm. One law firm singularly focused on the clients' experiences when dealing with difficult and often intensely emotional legal matters involving divorce and family law. As evidenced by so many glowing testimonials, clients benefit tremendously from the firm's exclusive family law and domestic relations representation; the attorneys' collective years of legal experience and litigation practice; the legal team's weekly meetings and strategy sessions; and the firm's transparent billing policy.

Since its formation, the Law Offices of Scott David Stewart has earned the trust and respect of nearly 2,000 clients in cases ranging from relatively simple marital dissolutions to those involving complex property divisions, contested child custody issues, parental visitation matters, and child relocation disputes.

Scott David Stewart loves his home state of Arizona where he mentors children and counsels families dealing with tough legal issues. When he's not working, mentoring, counseling, and writing books, the author spends his free time breaking a sweat at the local gym, golfing in the warm Arizona sunshine, volunteering at his church, and spending time with his family and friends.

Made in the USA
Lexington, KY
09 December 2019